Art
of
Successful Living

Published by
Lotus Press

Art
of
Successful Living

Vimal Kapoor

Lotus PRESS

4263/3, Ansari Road,
Darya Ganj, New Delhi-110002

Lotus Press

4263/3, Ansari Road, Darya Ganj, New Delhi- 110002
Ph.: 32903912, 23280047
E-mail: lotus_press@sify.com
www.lotuspress.co.in

Art of Successful Living
© 2008, Lotus Press
ISBN 81-8382-174-X

Published by: Lotus Press, New Delhi.
Typeset by: Naissance, New Delhi.
Printed at: Anand Sons, Delhi.

PREFACE

Life is full of challenges and opportunities. These challenges sometimes provide good success to an individual and sometime one cannot grab the potential and this can cause many problems in one's life. Everybody wants to live a good and successful life but everyone cannot necessarily have a good life. Physical wealth is not the only thing which can guarantee a good life. There are scores of people who have great wealth but still feel that they are not successful at all. There cannot be one certain rule for successful living but there are some methods which can help an individual to live a comparatively better and successful life.

This book is primarily meant to tell some methods to have a successful living. This is an attempt to provide the way of good living or what we simply call the *Art of Successful Living*. To feel good from within is the most important thing and we can start this by some pranic healing, meditation and yoga techniques. This book starts with the introductory chapter on the understanding of good living and tells the benefits of pranic healing followed by the importance of meditation and yoga in helping us to live a better life. The concept of *karma* and some religious thoughts can immensely help every individual in overcoming various problems.

If we harmonise ourselves with life and can understand that everything happens for a good cause, it will definitely help us in living a good and peaceful life. These topics are prominently mentioned in this book. Religious thoughts are very important in helping an individual in many ways. Some modern thoughts on good living find mention here. This book is an initiative in providing useful tips to have a good and successful living and we expect that the book will find its due place among the readers.

Author

CONTENTS

Understanding of Good Living

Life is no thing. Life is an endless chaos of possibilities. By selecting some of those possibilities we weave a web determined by a pattern we cannot know beforehand. It is this selection of possibilities, or the weaving, or the woven web, which people mistakenly look as life. Yet realise that life remains for ever untouched by the weaving of man. We make our understanding of life what we will, but life in itself is a transcendent state of flux having no form, and yet giving rise to all forms.

Sources of Good Living

Pranic healing

Pranic healing is an energy healing technique based on the overall structure of the human body. According to the precepts of pranic healing, our body is actually composed of two parts: the visible physical body, and the invisible energy body called the bioplasmic body or aura. The visible physical body is that part of the human body that we see, touch, and are most acquainted with. Our aura is that invisible luminous energy body, which interpenetrates the visible physical body and extends beyond it. Traditionally, clairvoyants and energy healing practitioners call this energy body the etheric body or etheric double.

Pranic healing is an ancient science and art of healing that utilises prana or life energy and the chakras or energy centre to heal diseased energy levels. The healing process involves the manipulation of the patient's chakras, *ki* and *aura*. It has also been called medical qigong (*ki* 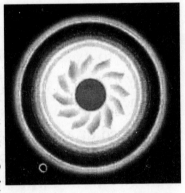 kung or *ki* healing), psychic healing, vitalic healing, therapeutic touch, laying of the hand, magnetic healing, faith healing, and charismatic healing.

Two basic laws of Pranic healing

Pranic healing is based on two laws: The law of self-recovery and the law of prana or life energy. These laws are quite obvious but strangely they are usually the least noticed or least remembered by most people. It is through these basic laws that rapid or miraculous healing occurs.

1. *Law of Self-Recovery*

In general, the body is capable of healing itself at a certain rate. If a person has a wound or burn, the body will heal itself and recover within a few days to a week. In other words, even if you do not apply antibiotic on the wound or burn, the body will repair or heal itself. At the present moment, there is no medicine available for the treatment of viral infection. But even if a person has cough or cold due to viral infection, the body will recover generally in one or two weeks without medication.

2. *Law of Life Energy*

For life to exist, the body must have prana, *chi* or life energy. The healing process can be accelerated by increasing life energy on the affected part(s) and on the entire body.

In chemistry, electrical energy is sometimes used as a catalyst to increase the rate of chemical reaction. Light can affect chemical reaction. This is the basis for photography. In electrolysis, electricity is used to catalyse or produce chemical reaction. In pranic healing, prana or life energy serves as the catalyst to accelerate the rate of biochemical reactions involved in the natural healing process of the body. When pranic energy is applied to the affected part of the body, the rate of recovery or healing increases tremendously.

What we call miraculous healing is nothing more than increasing the rate of self-recovery of the body. There is nothing supernatural or paranormal about pranic healing. It is simply based on natural laws that most people are not aware of.

Although science is not able to detect and measure life energy or prana, it does not mean that prana does not exist or does not affect the health and well-being of the body. In ancient times, people were not aware of the existence of electricity, its properties and practical uses. But this does not mean that electricity does not exist. One's ignorance does not change reality; it simply alters the perception of reality, resulting in misperception and misconception of what is  and what is not, what can be done and what cannot be done.

Children have more life energy than elderly people do. You notice that they move a lot from morning to night, hardly getting tired at all. When suffering from a fracture, who heals faster—the child or the elderly? The broken bone of a child heals very fast while that of an elderly heals very slowly; sometimes, it will not even heal at all.

Prana or *Ki*

Prana or *ki* is that life energy which keeps the body alive and healthy. In Greek it is called 'pneuma', in Polynesian 'mana', and in Hebrew 'ruah', which means 'breath of life'. The healer projects prana or life energy or 'the breath of life' to the patient, thereby, healing the patient. It is through this process that this so-called 'miraculous healing' is accomplished.

Basically, there are three major sources of prana: solar prana, air prana and ground prana. Solar prana is prana from sunlight. It invigorates the whole body and promotes good health. It can be obtained by sunbathing or exposure to sunlight for about five to ten minutes and by drinking water that has been exposed to sunlight. Prolonged exposure or too much solar prana would harm the whole physical body since it is quite potent.

Prana contained in the air is called air prana or air vitality globule. Air prana is absorbed by the lungs through breathing and is also absorbed directly by the energy centre of the bioplasmic body. These energy centre are called chakras. More air prana can be absorbed by deep slow rhythmic breathing than by short shallow breathing. It can also be absorbed through the pores of the skin by persons who have undergone certain training.

Prana contained in the ground is called ground prana or ground vitality globule. This is absorbed through the soles of the feet. This is done automatically and unconsciously. Walking barefoot increases the amount of ground prana absorbed by the body. One can learn to consciously draw in more ground prana to increase one's vitality, capacity to do more work, and ability to think more clearly.

Water absorbs prana from sunlight, air, and ground

that it comes in contact with. Plants and trees absorb prana from sunlight, air, water, and ground. Men and animals obtain prana from sunlight, air, ground, water, and food. Fresh food contains more prana than preserved food.

Prana can also be projected to another person for healing. Persons with a lot of excess prana tend to make other people around them feel better and livelier. However, those who are depleted tend to unconsciously absorb prana from other people. You may have encountered persons who tend to make you feel tired or drained for no apparent reason at all.

Certain trees, such alpine trees or old and gigantic healthy trees, exude a lot of excess prana. Tired or sick people benefit much by lying down or resting underneath these trees. Better results can be obtained by verbally requesting the being of the tree to help the sick person get well. Anyone can also learn to consciously absorb prana from these trees through the palms, such that the body would tingle and become numb because of the tremendous amount of prana absorbed. This skill can be acquired after only a few sessions of practice.

Certain areas or places tend to have more prana than others. Some of these highly energised areas tend to become healing centre.

During bad weather conditions, many people get sick not only because of the changes in temperature but also because of the decrease in solar and air prana (life energy). Thus, a lot of people feel mentally and physically sluggish or become susceptible to infectious diseases. This can be counteracted by consciously absorbing prana or *ki* from the air and the ground. It has been clairvoyantly observed that there is more prana during daytime than at night. Prana reaches a very low level at about three or four in the morning.

Aura

Clairvoyants, with the use of their psychic faculties, have observed that every person is surrounded and interpenetrated by a luminous energy body called the bioplasmic body or aura. Just like the visible physical body, it has a head, two eyes, two arms, etc. In other words, the bioplasmic body looks like the visible physical body. This is why clairvoyants call it the etheric double or etheric body.

The word 'bioplasmic' comes from 'bio', which means life and plasma, which is the fourth state of matter, the first three being: solid, liquid, and gas. Plasma is ionised gas or gas with positive and negative charged particles. This is not the same as blood plasma. Bioplasmic body means a living energy body made up of invisible subtle matter or etheric matter. To simplify the terminology, the term 'energy body' will be used to replace the word 'bioplasmic body'. Science, with the use of Kirlian photography, has rediscovered the energy body. With the aid of Kirlian photography, scientists have been able to study, observe, and take pictures of small bioplasmic articles like bioplasmic fingers, leaves, etc. It is through the energy body that prana or life energy is absorbed and distributed throughout the whole physical body.

Benefits of pranic healing

1. It can help parents bring down the temperature of their children suffering from high fever in just a few hours and heal it in a day or two in most cases.

2. It can relieve headaches, gas pains, toothaches, and muscle pains almost immediately in most cases.

3. Cough and cold can usually be cured in a day or two. Loose bowel movement can be healed in a few hours in most cases.

4. Major illnesses such as eye, liver, kidney, and heart problems can be relieved in a few sessions and healed in a few months in many cases.

5. It increases the rate of healing by three times or more than the normal rate of healing. These are some of the few things that pranic healing can do. All of these assume that the healer has attained a certain degree of proficiency.

Pranic healing is easy to learn

Any healthy person with an average intelligence, an average ability to concentrate, an open but discriminating mind, and a certain degree of persistence can learn pranic healing in a relatively short period. Learning pranic healing is easier than learning to play the piano or painting. It is as easy as learning to drive. Its basic principles and techniques can be learned in a few sessions. Like driving, pranic healing requires much practice and time to achieve a certain degree of proficiency.

Some Healing Principles

Proper diet

Proper diet simply refers to pure and nutritious food. In general meat, and in particular pork, contains a lot of dirty grayish energy and therefore it is better to avoid them. Fresh vegetables and fruits are nutritious, pure and luminous. They carry a lot of pranic energy or life force. Taking one to two grams of bee pollen daily is also very beneficial. Bee pollen is physically nutritious and contains a lot of life force.

Proper breathing

Breathing is of two types, the correct way and the incorrect way. The correct way is abdominal breathing and the incorrect way is chest breathing. It is the diaphragm, which enables the lungs to expand and to contract. The lungs by themselves do not have the capacity to expand in order to draw in air, or to contract in order to expel used-up air. With abdominal breathing, the abdomen is slightly pushed out during inhalation, causing the diaphragm to be pulled down, which enables the lungs to draw in more air. During exhalation, the abdomen is slightly pulled in, causing the diaphragm to be pushed up, which enables the lungs to exhale more used-up air. Also, more pranic energy is drawn in during inhalation and more used-up energy is expelled during exhalation.

With chest breathing, the abdomen is pulled in during inhalation, causing the diaphragm to be pushed up resulting in less air being drawn in. During exhalation, the abdomen is pushed out, causing the diaphragm to be pulled down in less air being expelled. Prolonged chest breathing also tends to congest the front heart chakra, resulting in chest pain and difficulty in breathing.

Proper exercise

Exercising has a cleansing effect—physically and etherically. Physically, waste matter and toxins are eliminated through sweating. When a person is exercising, the auras of the energy body pulsate; whitish gray light or used-up energy is expelled and fresh pranic energy is drawn in. The chakras, the meridians and the organs are cleansed of used-up energy and diseased energy. Blood and pranic circulations are greatly improved by regular exercise. The body feels better and lighter after exercising. Regular physical exercise is a must to maintain a clean, highly vitalised, healthy body.

Tai Chi, chi kung exercise, hatha yoga, dancing, martial arts, sports, jogging, hiking or brisk walking, if done regularly, have very good effects on the body. The left and right parts of the body should preferably be in balance, while exercising. Otherwise, the part of the body, which is not sufficiently exercised will become weaker and partially congested, which may manifest as pain or discomfort. Fifteen to thirty minutes of exercise daily is sufficient.

Proper etheric hygiene

Proper hygiene consists of physical hygiene, etheric hygiene, emotional hygiene, and mental hygiene.

Smoking is a very unhygienic habit. Smokers have unclean physical as well as etheric bodies. In the case of chain smokers, the etheric body is polluted with dirty brown energy, which partially blocks most of the meridians, thereby weakening the physical body in general. Since the back meridian in the spine is partially blocked; the back solar plexus chakra, the meng mein chakra, and the basic chakra tend to become congested and overactivated, thereby making the smoker susceptible to hypertension. The front heart chakra is partially affected, making the habitually heavy smoker susceptible to heart problems, since the front heart chakra is closely connected to the back heart chakra.

Habitual drinking of liquor with high alcohol content is etherically unhygienic. It makes the etheric body unclean and gross. Drug addiction impurifies and damages the etheric body, making the addict susceptible to undesirable external psychic influences.

In certain lands the etheric energy is unclean. This is clairvoyantly seen as light grayish energy coming out of the ground. If the reclaimed land has been dumped with garbage, then the area is etherically impure or polluted. These areas, in the long run, tend to adversely affect the physical and psychological health of its residents. It is just like living in a highly polluted city.

Certain places are likewise etherically quite unclean like hospitals, funeral parlors, cemeteries and others. Relatively weak persons are advised to take a shower using water and salt after visiting any one of these places.

If a very sickly person has used a room for a long period of time, then the room is filled with diseased energy, and it must be cleansed. If a room or a house has been occupied by a negative or psychologically disturbed person, then the room is not physically and psychologically conducive to one's well being. Etherically unclean rooms can be cleansed by using water and salt, burning sandalwood incense, praying, exposing to sunlight, besides others.

Objects can also be etherically contaminated. As a general guideline, it is better to avoid lending one's personal things to others to avoid etheric contamination. Likewise, it is advisable to avoid using the personal things of other people.

When buying or accepting second-hand things, especially pieces of jewelry, it is advisable to know the condition of the previous owner(s) since the characteristics of the previous owner are impregnated in his personal belongings. If the previous owner was quite sickly or very negative, then possessing a second-hand item from him or her would be unhealthy and unlucky.

One can also be contaminated when interacting with others. When interacting with a sick person, you may tend to feel depleted since the sick person may subconsciously absorb some of your healthy pranic energy and you may also accidentally absorb some of the diseased energy.

It is a healthy practice to go to the beach regularly about once a month or once every two months. Seawater has a cleansing effect on the energy body. The body is highly energised with prana from the fresh air, sunlight, and ground.

Emotional and mental hygiene

Proper emotional and mental hygiene consists of internal and external hygiene. Internal emotional and mental hygiene simply means proper emotions and proper thoughts. Positive emotions and thoughts like happiness, kindness, joy, enthusiasm, and others tend to have beneficial effects psychologically, etherically, and physically.

In many instances, negative emotion is one of the critical factors, if not the most critical factor, in severe ailments. Harboring or explosively expressing negative may manifest as glaucoma, migraine headache, acute sinusitis, hyperthyroidism, respiratory ailments like asthma, heart ailments, diabetes, gastric or intestinal ulcer, high cholesterol, infected liver, constipation, twisted intestine, damaged kidneys, hypertension, rheumatoid arthritis, cancer and others.

When negative emotions are accompanied by negative thoughts, the upper chakra like the throat, ajna, forehead or crown chakra will also be affected. This may manifest as hyperthyroidism, acute sinusitis, migraine headache, glaucoma, epilepsy, and others.

When negative emotions are accompanied by expressed or inhibited physical aggression, the lower chakra like the meng main chakra, and the basic chakra will also be affected. This may manifest as hypertension, damaged kidneys, herniated disk, skin ailments, rheumatoid arthritis, blood ailments, and others.

External emotional and mental hygiene means proper company, since emotions and thoughts are transmissible. Negative emotions and thoughts are infectious.

Therefore, after to a person with psychological problems, one may feel depressed and physically exhausted. Prolonged interaction with this type of persons may manifest as physical ailment(s).

It is preferably to be sexually selective, since it is very easy to be etherically and psychologically contaminated through indiscriminate sexual interactions. After such an interaction, it is advisable to clean oneself physically, etherically, emotionally, and mentally.

Food should preferably be handled and prepared by persons in good health and bad energy can easily be transmitted to food and objects.

Interacting with people who are optimistic, enthusiastic and very healthy is very psychologically and etherically beneficial.

Forgiveness and loving – kindness

Some severe ailments are emotional in origin. Some patients have so much deep-seated hurt or resentment towards certain person(s). Although pranic healing does greatly improve the condition of the patient, the rate of healing would be much faster if the patient consciously exerts an effort to forgive those who may have actually or imaginarily hurt him or her. The act of forgiving is therapeutic and is necessary for good health. It helps normalise the other affected chakras.

Proper human relationships

Cruelty to fellow beings and to animals is one of the major causes of severe painful ailments. If one repeatedly causes pain to others, then one will also harvest intense pain in the form of severe ailment. If one repeatedly deprives others of physical sustenance (income, money or food), then one will also be deprived of physical sustenance. This may manifest as severe lung ailments wherein one keeps gasping for life (sustenance). The affected body will gradually wilt. This will also have adverse financial effects.

Even prophets are not exempted from the law of karma. Negative karma can be neutralised by learning the lesson that has to be learned, using the law of forgiveness and the law of mercy. Avoid cruelty and show kindness to others; this is a major key to good health, to happiness, and to avoiding severe painful ailments.

Proper livelihood

The nature of the work, the psychological condition of co-workers, and the working overall environment of a person do affect considerably the health of the worker. In this so-called modern developed world, there is too much stress or tension.

In other words, there is a lot of work pressure, hurriedness, worry and anxiety, irritation, anger, and hurt feelings, excessive aggressiveness, bullying and harassment.

Severe stress or tension, in the long run, causes the solar plexus chakra and the other chakras to malfunction. This may manifest as gastric ulcer, heart ailments, hyperthyroidism, severe sinusitis, migraine headache, malfunctioning liver, damaged kidneys, general weakness, depression and others.

Meditation would definitely help a lot in coping with stressful conditions. In certain cases, where the meditation has certain degree of limitation, it may be wiser to change for a better job or a livelihood that is less demanding and with saner working condition.

The psychological state of co-workers is also important since stress is physically very infectious. People under great stress radiate stress energy to the surrounding people through their chakras and auras. Consciously or subconsciously, they transfer a great bulk of their stress energy by being nasty and rude to others. This type of behaviour is unacceptable and quite uncivilised. In the future, such behaviour will be considered coarse and barbaric. It is very impolite and improper to dump one's psychic faces on others. The proper way to dispose of stress energy is to meditate, to do self-pranic healing or to have pranic treatment. Work productivity can be improved substantially by letting executives and workers have regular pranic treatment.

Prolonged stress is a psychological ailment, which will adversely affect the physical body. In more developed countries, stress is a national epidemic. It is the right of each worker to have not only a physically safe working environment but also a psychologically healthy environment to work in. It is just a matter of time that this basic human right will be recognised and respected.

Self pranic healing for stress

With people who are undergoing a lot of stress, the solar plexus chakra is very congested and over activated. The solar plexus chakra is filled with dirty and red energy. The other chakras are also affected.

Apply self-localised sweeping on the front solar plexus

chakra for thirty times or more. The sweeping should be done slowly and in counterclockwise motion. Throw the dirty energy to the basin with water and salt. This will substantially reduce the stress.

Do keep pranic breathing for twelve cycles or more in order to further normalise the solar plexus chakra, to achieve inner calmness, and to recharge one-self. Or do meditation on Twin Hearts.

Repeat the procedure several times a day if necessary. Meditation on Twin Hearts is preferably done not more than once or twice a day since it may cause pranic congestion.

If stress is severe, contact an advanced pranic healer for regular preventive pranic psychotherapy treatment.

Proper lifestyle

The lifestyle of a person is an important health factor. Undesirable habits and excessiveness like smoking, alcoholism, drug abuse, excessive work and excessive fun are to be avoided.

Meditation and Yoga for Good Living

What is meditation?

Meditation describes a state of concentrated attention on some object of thought or awareness. It usually involves turning the attention inward to a single point of reference. The benefits of the practice can engender a higher state of consciousness. Meditation is recognised as a component of eastern religions, where it has been practiced for over 5,000 years. Different meditative disciplines encompass a wide range of spiritual and/or psychophysical practices which can emphasise development of either a high degree of mental concentration, or the apparent converse, mental quiescence.

The word meditation comes from the Latin meditatio, which originally indicated every type of physical or intellectual exercise, then later evolved into the more specific meaning "contemplation." Eastern spiritual teachings, including meditation, have been adapted and increasingly practiced in Western culture.

An ordinary person may consider meditation as a worship or prayer. But it is not so. Meditation means awareness. Whatever you do with awareness is meditation. "Watching your breath" is meditation; listening to the birds is meditation. As long as these activities are free from any other distraction to the mind, it is effective meditation.

Meditation is not a technique but a way of life. Meditation means 'a cessation of the thought process'. It describes a state of consciousness, when the mind is free of scattered thoughts and various patterns. The observer (one who is doing meditation) realises that all the activity of the mind is reduced to one.

A Tibetan Lama was being monitored on a brain scan machine by a scientist wishing to test physiological functions during deep meditation. The scientist said: "Very good Sir. The machine shows that you are able to go very deep in brain relaxation, and that validates your meditation". "No", said the Lama, "This (pointing to his brain) validates the machine!"

These days it is commonly understood to mean some form of spiritual practice where one sits down with eyes closed and empties the mind to attain inner peace, relaxation or even an experience of God. Some people use the term as "my gardening is my meditation" or for jogging or art or music, hence creating confusion or misunderstanding.

The word meditation is derived from two Latin words: meditari (to think, to dwell upon, to exercise the mind) and mederi (to heal). Its Sanskrit derivation 'medha' means wisdom.

Many years ago meditation was considered something just not meant for modern people, but now it has become very popular with all types of people. Published scientific and medical evidence has proved its benefits, but it still needs to be much understood.

Traditionally, the classical yoga texts, describe that to attain true states of meditation one must go through several stages. After the necessary preparation of personal and social code, physical position, breath control, and relaxation come the more advanced stages of concentration, contemplation, and then ultimately absorption. But that does not mean that one must perfect any one stage before moving onto the next. The Integral yoga approach is simultaneous application of a little of all stages together.

Commonly today, people can mean any one of these stages when they refer to the term meditation. Some schools only teach concentration techniques, some relaxation, and others teach free form contemplative activities like just sitting and awaiting absorption. Some call it meditation without giving credence to yoga for fear of being branded 'eastern'. But yoga is not something eastern or western as it is universal in its approach and application.

With regular practice of a balanced series of techniques, the energy of the body and mind can be liberated and the quality of consciousness can be expanded. This is not a subjective claim but is now being investigated by the scientists and being shown by an empirical fact.

Different forms of meditation

Meditation has been defined as: "self-regulation of attention, in the service of self-inquiry, in the here and now." The various techniques of meditation can be classified according to their focus. Some focus on the field or background perception and experience, also called "mindfulness;" others focus on a preselected specific object, and are called "concentrative" meditation. There are also techniques that shift between the field and the object.

In mindfulness meditation, the meditator sits comfortably and silently, centering attention by focusing awareness on an object or process (either the breath, a sound: a mantra, koan or riddle evoking questions; a visualisation, or an exercise). The meditator is usually encouraged to maintain an open focus: shifting freely from one perception to the next clear your mind of all that bothers you no thoughts that can distract you from reality or your personal being. No thought, image or sensation is considered an intrusion. The meditator, with a 'no effort' attitude, is asked to remain in the here and now. Using the focus as an 'anchor' brings the subject constantly back to the present, avoiding cognitive analysis or fantasy regarding the contents of awareness, and increasing tolerance and relaxation of secondary thought processes.

Concentration meditation is used in most religions and spiritual practices. Whereas in mindfulness meditation there is an open focus, in concentration meditation the meditator holds attention on a particular object (e.g., a repetitive prayer) while minimising distractions; bringing the mind back to concentrate on the chosen object. In some traditions, such as Vipassana, mindfulness and concentration are combined.

Meditation can be practiced while walking or doing simple repetitive tasks. Walking meditation helps to break down habitual automatic mental categories, "thus regaining the primary nature of perceptions and events, focusing attention on the process while disregarding its purpose or final outcome." In a form of meditation using visualisation, such as Chinese Qi Gong, the practitioner concentrates on flows of energy (Qi) in the body, starting in the abdomen and then circulating through the body, until dispersed. Some meditative traditions, such as yoga or tantra, are common to several religions or occur outside religious contexts.

Types of Meditation–Classification

All the meditation techniques can be grouped into two basic approaches:

1.   Concentrative meditation, and
2.   Mindfulness meditation.

Concentrative meditation

Concentrative meditation focuses the attention on the breath, an image, or a sound (mantra), in order to still the mind and allow a greater awareness and clarity to emerge. This is like a zoom lens in a camera; we narrow our focus to a selected field.

The simplest form of concentrative meditation is to sit quietly and focus the attention on the breath. Yoga and meditation practitioners believe that there is a direct correlation between one's breath and one's state of the mind. For example, when a person is anxious, frightened, agitated, or distracted, the breath will tend to be shallow,

rapid, and uneven. On the other hand, when the mind is calm, focused, and composed, the breath will tend to be slow, deep, and regular.

Focusing the mind on the continuous rhythm of inhalation and exhalation provides a natural object of meditation. As you focus your awareness on the breath, your mind becomes absorbed in the rhythm of inhalation and exhalation. As a result, your breathing will become slower and deeper, and the mind becomes more tranquil and aware.

Mindfulness meditation

Mindfulness meditation, "involves opening the attention to become aware of the continuously passing parade of sensations and feelings, images, thoughts, sounds, smells, and so forth without becoming involved in thinking about them."

The person sits quietly and simply witnesses whatever goes through the mind, not reacting or becoming involved with thoughts, memories, worries, or images. This helps to gain a more calm, clear, and non-reactive  state of mind. Mindfulness meditation can be likened to a wide-angle lens. Instead of narrowing your sight to a selected field as in concentrative meditation, here you will be aware of the entire field.

Healing power of meditation

Research has shown that Meditation can contribute to an individual's psychological and physiological well-being. This is accomplished as Meditation brings the brainwave pattern into an alpha state, which is a level of consciousness that promotes the healing state.

There is scientific evidence that Meditation can reduce blood pressure and relieve pain and stress. When used in combination with biofeedback, Meditation enhances the effectiveness of biofeedback.

One prominent report says: "In our practice we use meditative techniques to enhance immune functioning in cancer, AIDS, and autoimmune patients. We also use meditation in conjunction with neuro-feedback to normalise brain rhythms and chemistry in alcohol and drug addiction, as well as other addictive conditions. Almost all of our patients use meditative techniques in learning self-regulation for disorders such as anxiety and hypertension, and for stress management. We consider meditation a recommended practice for anyone seeking high-level wellness."

Benefits of Meditation

Physical benefits

- Deep rest–as measured by decreased metabolic rate,

lower heart rate, and reduced work load of the heart.

- Lowered levels of cortisol and lactate–two chemicals associated with stress.

- Reduction of free radicals–unstable oxygen molecules that can cause tissue damage. They are now thought to be a major factor in aging and in many diseases.

- Decreased high blood pressure.

- Higher skin resistance. Low skin resistance is correlated with higher stress and anxiety levels.

- Drop in cholesterol levels. High cholesterol is associated with cardiovascular disease.

- Improved flow of air to the lungs resulting in easier breathing. This has been very helpful to asthma patients.

- Younger biological age. On standard measures of aging, long-term Transcendental Meditation (TM) practitioners (more than five years) measured 12 years younger than their chronological age.

- Higher levels of DHEAS in the elderly. An additional sign of youthfulness through Transcendental Meditation (TM); lower levels of DHEAS are associated with aging.

Psychological benefits

- Increased brain wave coherence. Harmony of brain wave activity in different parts of the brain is associated with greater creativity, improved moral reasoning, and higher IQ.

- Decreased anxiety.
- Decreased depression.
- Decreased irritability and moodiness.
- Improved learning ability and memory.
- Increased self-actualization.
- Increased feelings of vitality and rejuvenation.
- Increased happiness.
- Increased emotional stability.

Health Conditions that are Benefited by Meditation

Drug addiction

The Transcendental Meditation technique has proven to be a successful coping strategy in helping to deal with drug addiction, a useful tool in psycho-neuro-immunology (PNI) by helping to control the immune system, and an effective manager of stress and pain.

Prolonging life expectancy

A strong link has also been established between the practice of TM and longevity. Only two factors have been scientifically determined to actually extend life: caloric restriction and lowering of the body's core temperature. Meditation has been shown to lower core body temperature.

Stress control

Most of the people who get on meditation do so because of its beneficial effects on stress. Stress refers to any or all the various pressures experienced in life. These can stem from work, family, illness, or environment and can contribute to such conditions as anxiety, hypertension, and heart disease. How an individual sees things and how he or she handles them makes a big difference in terms of how much stress he or she experiences.

Research has shown that hormones and other biochemical compounds in the blood indicative of stress tend to decrease during TM practice. These changes also stabilise over time, so that a person is actually less stressed biochemically during daily activity.

This reduction of stress translates directly into a reduction of anxiety and tension. Literally dozens of studies have shown this.

Pain management

Chronic pain can systematically erode the quality of life. Although great strides are being made in traditional medicine to treat recurring pain, treatment is rarely as simple as prescribing medication or surgery.

Anxiety decreases the threshold for pain and pain causes anxiety. The result is a vicious cycle. Compared with people who feel relaxed, those under stress experience pain more intensely and become even more stressed, which aggravates their pain. Meditation breaks this cycle.

Childbirth preparation classes routinely teach pregnant women deep breathing exercises to minimise the pain and anxiety of labour. Few call it breath meditation, but that's what it is.

Meditative techniques are also a key element in the Arthritis Self-help Course at Stanford University. More than 100,000 people with arthritis have taken the 12-hour course and learned meditation-style relaxation exercises as part of a comprehensive self-care programme. Graduates report a 15 to 20 per cent reduction in pain.

In one study overseen by Dr. Kabat-Zinn, 72 per cent of the patients with chronic pain conditions achieved at least a 33 per cent reduction after participating in an eight-week period of mindful meditation, while 61 per cent of the pain patients achieved at least a 50 per cent reduction. Additionally, these people perceived their bodies as being 30 per cent less problematic, suggesting an overall improvement in self-esteem and positive views regarding their bodies.

Meditation may not eliminate pain, but it helps people cope more effectively.

Cancer and other chronic illness

Meditation and other approaches to deep relaxation help cancer patients so they can figure out how they'd like to handle the illness and proceed with life. Dr. Ainslie Meares, an Australian psychiatrist who uses meditation with cancer patients, studied seventy-three patients who had attended at least twenty–sessions of intensive meditation, and wrote: "Nearly all such patients can expect significant reduction of anxiety and depression, together with much less discomfort and pain. There is reason to expect a 10 per cent chance of quite remarkable slowing of the rate of growth of the tumor, and a 50 per cent chance of greatly improved quality of life."

Heart disease

Meditation is a key component of Ornish therapy, the only treatment scientifically proven to reverse heart disease.

High blood pressure

As soon as Dr. Benson learned that TM reliably reduced blood pressure in meditators, he taught the relaxation response to 36 people with moderately elevated blood pressure. After several weeks of practice, their average blood pressure declined significantly, reducing their risk of stroke and heart attack.

Infertility

Couples dealing with infertility may become depressed, anxious and angry. To help them cope, Alice D. Domar, Ph.D., a psychologist at the Mind/Body Medical Institute, taught the relaxation response to one group of infertile couples. Compared with a similar group of infertile couples who did not learn deep relaxation, the meditators experienced less distress, – and were more likely to get pregnant.

Psoriasis

This disease causes scaly red patches on the skin. A pilot study at Dr. Kabat-Zinn's clinic suggests that compared with the skin patches of people with psoriasis who receive only standard medical therapy, the skin patches of those who also meditate clear up more quickly.

Respiratory crises

Asthma, emphysema and chronic obstructive pulmonary disease (COPD) all restrict breathing and raise fears of suffocation, which in turn makes breathing even more difficult. Studies at Dr. Kabat-Zinn's clinic show that when people with these respiratory conditions learn breath meditation, they have fewer respiratory crises.

Premenstrual Syndrome (PMS), Tension Headaches

Meditation can ease physical complaints such as premenstrual syndrome (PMS), tension headaches and other common health problems.

Meditation gives people a psychological buffer so that life's hectic pace doesn't knock them out. Practicing meditation is like taking a vacation once or twice a day. When you nurture yourself, you accrue tremendous spin-off benefits.

For example, when you are under high stress, it can worsen symptoms of PMS because stress can cause the muscle tension associated with PMS complaints such as fatigue, soreness and aching. On the other hand, when you meditate regularly, you dramatically reduce your body's response to stress, and that can ease the discomfort associated with PMS. The results may not be apparent for several months. You will probably need to meditate regularly for several months before your body responds positively.

Irritable Bowel Syndrome, Ulcers, and Insomnia

Meditation can also improve irritable bowel syndrome, ulcers, and insomnia, among other stress-related conditions. Eighty per cent of the people who use meditation to relieve insomnia are successful.

Meditation can help prevent or treat stress-related complaints such as anxiety, headaches and bone, muscle and joint problems. Meditation also provides an inner sense of clarity and calm, and that, in itself, may help ward-off certain illnesses.

Fibromyalgia

According to one study, meditation may relieve the discomfort of fibromyalgia, a condition that causes fatigue and intensely painful "trigger points." When 77 men and women with fibromyalgia followed a ten-week stress-reduction programme using meditation, all reported that their symptoms improved. And half described their improvements as "moderate to marked."

Psychological Benefits of Meditation

Meditation can help most people feel less anxious and

more in control. The awareness that meditation brings can also be a source of personal insight and self-understanding.

Handling repressed memories and enjoying life

Meditation may lead to a breakdown of screen memories so that early childhood abuse episodes and other traumas suddenly flood the mind, making the patient temporarily more anxious until these traumas are healed. Many so-called meditation exercises are actually forms of imagery and visualisation that are extraordinarily useful in healing old traumas, confronting death anxieties, finishing 'old business', learning to forgive, and enhancing self-esteem.

"Meditation frees persons from tenacious preoccupation with the past and future and allows them to fully experience life's precious moments", says a study, at the Insight Meditation Center and lay dharma teacher of insight meditation in suburban Boston.

Many men and women tend to live in a state of perpetual motion and expectation that prevents them from appreciating the gifts that each moment gives us. We live life in a state of insufficiency, waiting for a mother to love us, for a father to be kind to us, for the perfect job or home, for Prince Charming to come along or to become a perfect person. It's a mythology that keeps us from being whole.

Meditation is a humble process that gently returns us to the now of our lives and allows us to wake up and re-evaluate the way that we live our lives. We realise that the only thing missing is mindfulness, and that's what we practice.

Depression

Feelings of helplessness, hopelessness and isolation are hallmarks of depression–the nation's most prevalent mental health problem. Meditation increases self-confidence and feelings of connection to others. Many studies have shown that depressed people feel much better after eliciting the relaxation response.

Panic attacks

Sometimes anxiety becomes paralysing and people feel (wrongly) that they are about to suffer some horrible fate. Panic attacks are often treated with drugs, but studies show that if people who are prone to panic attacks begin focused, meditative breathing the instant they feel the first signs of an episode, they are less likely to have a full-blown panic attack.

Spiritual benefits of meditation

The longer an individual practices meditation, the greater the likelihood that his or her goals and efforts will shift toward personal and spiritual growth. Many individuals who initially learn meditation for its self-regulatory aspects find that as their practice deepens they are drawn more and more into the realm of the "spiritual."

Illness in general

Many of Nature's cures–acupressure, aromatherapy, biofeedback, exercise, heat and cold therapies, massage therapy, music therapy, tai chi and chi gong, visualisation, guided imagery and self-hypnosis and yoga incorporate elements of meditation.

The Concept of Yoga

Yoga is a way of life, an art of righteous living or an integrated system for the benefit of the body, mind and inner spirit. This art originated, was perfected and practiced in India thousands of years ago. The references to yoga are available in 'Upanishads' and 'Puranas' composed by Indian Aryans in the later Vedic and post–Vedic period. The main credit for systematising yoga goes to Patanjali who wrote 'Yoga Sutra', two thousand years ago. He described the principles of the full eight fold yogic discipline. He composed the treatise in brief code words known as 'Sutras'. 'Yoga Sutra' is the most important basic

text on Yoga. It is through this basic treatise that the essential message of yoga spread throughout the world.

Yoga has been defined as referring to "technologies or disciplines of asceticism and meditation which are thought to lead to spiritual experience and profound understanding or insight into the nature of existence." Yoga is also intimately connected to the religious beliefs and practices of the other Indian religions.

Outside India, Yoga is mostly associated with the practice of asanas (postures) of Hatha Yoga or as a form of exercise, although it has influenced the entire Indian religions family and other spiritual practices throughout the world.

Hindu texts discussing different aspects of yoga include the *Upanishads*, the *Bhagavad Gita*, the *Yoga Sutras of Patanjali*, the *Hatha Yoga Pradipika*, the *Shiva Samhita*, and many others.

Major branches of Yoga include: Hatha Yoga, Karma Yoga, Jnana Yoga, Bhakti Yoga, and Raja Yoga. Raja Yoga, established by the Yoga Sutras of Patanjali, and known simply as Yoga in the context of Hindu philosophy, is one of the six orthodox (âstika) schools of thought.

The four types of yoga: reaching towards the divine

In Hinduism, there are four main ways to reach towards the divine reality, whether the ultimate goal is a better life, union with the divine, or a release from life. The ways are called yoga, a word similar to the English term "yoke." And, just as yoke implies a burden or a discipline of actions, so too does yoga. Each yoga puts on its followers a set of actions that help lead the practitioner towards their goal. The yogas are: Jnana yoga, Bhakti yoga, Karma yoga, and Raja yoga. The first three are discussed in the *Bhagavad Gita*, while the fourth derives initially from the *Yoga Sutra*. These are all spiritual approaches to understanding the divine world; what we in the west generally term yoga—forms of physical exercise and control of the body—is properly known as Hatha yoga. It has no spiritual impact.

Janana Yoga

Janana means knowledge and this yoga is the path to understanding ultimate reality through knowledge. Of course, the reality the yogi (a practitioner of yoga) is trying to comprehend is the identity of atman (one's own soul) with Brahman (the creator and essence of the cosmos). And comprehension of this identity must happen not just at the intellectual level, but with every fibre of a person's being.

There are three main steps in Jnana yoga. The first is learning. The initiate is taught about the identity of atman and Brahman through instruction, study of holy writings, and so on. Once the intellectual understanding of the concept has been achieved, the yogi moves to the next level.

The second step is that of thinking. The yogi is taught to embody the teaching he has received. The teacher often encourages this process, for example, by pushing the student to think about the "I," "me," and "my" that always crop up in a person's speech. The goal of this stage is to bring the yogi to the ability to separate his/her eternal soul (the Self) from the temporary self within which it is encased.

The third step is to differentiate oneself from oneself. In other words, once it is understood that each individual's eternal atman is enclosed in a temporary body of maya, the goal is to relocate one's identity in the atman, rather than in the body and its temporary accompanying emotions and thoughts. In the initial stages of this process, the yogi begins to think of themselves in the third person. Rather than thinking, "I am taking a bath," they think, "Ram is taking a bath." A person thus becomes an observer of their temporary body, rather than its motivator. The ultimate aim is complete detachment of the eternal Self from the temporary one. Once this is achieved, then there is nothing that separates the Self (the atman) from Brahman.

Bhakti Yoga

This is the path of devotion to a god, or, more precisely, the path of the love of a god. A person thus centre on a god or goddess (such as Vishnu, Parvati, Ganesha) and expresses their love for him or her. The goal is not to just say "I love Shiva" or "I love Kali" or just to perform acts of love and worship, but to actually love them, to devote oneself to them as if they were a lover, a parent or one's child.

Bhakti takes many forms. It can be the constant repetition of the god's/goddess' name throughout the day  to enhance a person's awareness of the divine being's role in life. It can be the giving of gifts to the god at his temple, and the participation in worship of the god there. It can be pilgrimage to a site sacred to the goddess' life. The goal is thus not identity or unity, but nearness. Lovers are not one person, they are two people whose lives are intertwined. So too it is with the worshipper and their god.

Karma Yoga

This yoga aims to reverse the natural order workings of karma. Karma is generated by every action a person performs during their lives, and, it is the working out of karma that requires rebirth after death. So, Karma Yoga reasons, if a person could live without generating karma, then there would be nothing to cause rebirth.

This task is accomplished by detachment, namely, the detachment of one's Self (one's atman) from one's actions. This is done by removing all involvement, including one's intent, from their activity. This can be accomplished either through the knowledge of one's true Self (like Jnana Yoga) or by putting all the actions onto one's god (following a path similar to Bhakti Yoga).

Raja Yoga

Raja means "royal," so this is the royal yoga. This is essentially the path of meditation, that is, of being able to remove one's own consciousness from its awareness of this world of maya and to focus only on the ultimate reality of the cosmos' unity. This is quite difficult to accomplish, and there are eight stages that are designed as the simplest path. The difficulty is to overcome one's awareness first of their surroundings, and then of  their own body and its activities (such as breathing and the pumping of the heart).

Once this is accomplished then a person must take control of their mind and to focus it on one thing only, Brahman. The goal is achieved when through concentration and meditation, all separateness of the world of maya disappears and the unity of atman and Brahman appears.

Aim of Yoga is the attainment of the physical, mental

and spiritual health. Patanjali has recommended eight stages of Yoga discipline. They are:

1. Yamas– Yamas (abstentions or restrains)

2. Niyamas– Niyamas (observances)-austerities, purity, contentment, study, surrender of the ego

3. Asanas– Physical postures or exercises

4. Pranayama– Control of vital energy (Breathing control)

5. Partyahara– Withdrawal of the senses

6. Dharana– Concentration of the mind (Contemplation)

7. Dhyana– Meditation

8. Samadhi– Attainment of The super conscious state.

Yoga is a 5000 years old science whose teachings were first imparted not in a classroom or Gurukul, but on the battle field. In the epic *Mahabharata*, the sage, Lord Krishna is first said to have imparted the teachings of Yoga to his despondent student Arjuna. Around 1500 years later, another sage, Patanjali, went on to enunciate, for the benefit of humankind and eternity, the way to reach the summom bonum of life through a series of 195 aphorisms (sutras) in his epic treatise The Yoga Sutras of Patanjali.

Derived from the Sanskrit root "Yujir Yogey" meaning to unite, to yoke, to join, to put together, Yoga is not about mind over body. On the other hand, Yoga is about developing harmony between them. In Yoga, you use your mind to perceive (diagnose) and guide (heal) your body. Never control, let alone force it!

Yoga is a way of life, a conscious act, not a set or series of learning principles. The dexterity, grace, and poise you cultivate, as a matter of course, is the natural outcome of regular practice. You require no major effort. In fact trying hard will turn your practices into a humdrum, painful, even injurious routine and will eventually slow down your progress. Subsequently, and interestingly, the therapeutic effect of Yoga is the direct result of involving the mind totally in inspiring (breathing) the body to awaken.

Contrary to popular – or unpopular – perception, Yoga positions are not about how far you can reach to touch your toes or how many repetitions you can perform. It is all about paying attention to how your body feels; how it moves without that excruciating pain or agony! Yoga is all about breathing correctly about integrating that breath into your being. Conscious Yoga doesn't call for you to force or strain your never or sinew. Meaning to say, right Yoga is learning how to do things right, do less that gets you more!

Ironically, by doing less – correctly – Yoga enhances your strength, energy, vitality, flexibility and levels of endurance. Accordingly, your body and mind start to become more balanced until, eventually, you find it takes so much less energy to move through the day. Yes, any and everyone can do less…and get a lot, lot more!

Everyday people are reporting their wonderful experiences with Yoga, the transformation of being, taking you beyond the here and now. In one wonderful session of Yoga, people get to practice a number of things, some Yoga poses (asanas) breathing exercises (pranayama), meditation and chanting. In Yoga you get to learn basic terms like Mudras, Bandhas and Chakras. Best of all, Yoga is fun and relaxing while, at the same time, being delectably challenging to beginners. The intermediate and advanced students, who insist on continuing their practices, get more and more of the taste of this great 5000+ year old wondrous way of life. Yoga is for the body, mind and spirit. You learn to use your body, breath and mind to stretch, relax and energize yourself. So get up and go!

Yoga is all about feeling good; feel the blood surging through your veins, the energy pulsating through your nerves, the bliss coursing through your whole being.

Best of all, Yoga is apt for all, regardless of age, color, caste, creed or religion; from the healthiest to the sickest, from the richest to the poorest, from the whitest to the blackest. And here are some of the specific – and immense – benefits of yoga:

At the outset, we must understand what we can gain out of this wonderful practice. More importantly, yoga is extremely effective in:

Increasing flexibility

Yoga has positions that act upon the various joints of the body including those joints that are never really on the 'radar screen' let alone exercised.

Increasing lubrication of the joints, ligaments and tendons

Likewise, the well-researched yoga positions exercise the different tendons and ligaments of the body.

Surprisingly it has been found that the body which may have been quite rigid starts experiencing a remarkable flexibility in even those parts which have not been consciously work upon. Why? It is here that the remarkable research behind yoga positions proves its mettle. Seemingly unrelated "non strenuous" yoga positions act upon certain parts of the body in an interrelated manner. When done together, they work in harmony to create a situation where flexibility is attained relatively easily.

Massaging of all organs of the Body

Yoga is perhaps the only form of activity which massages all the internal glands and organs of the body in a thorough manner, including those – such as the prostate – that hardly get externally stimulated during our entire lifetime. Yoga acts in a wholesome manner on the various body parts. This stimulation and massage of the organs in turn benefits us by keeping away disease and providing a forewarning at the first possible instance of a likely onset of disease or disorder.

One of the far-reaching benefits of yoga is the uncanny sense of awareness that it develops in the practitioner of an impending health disorder or infection. This in turn enables the person to take pre-emptive corrective action.

Complete Detoxification

By gently stretching muscles and joints as well as massaging the various organs, yoga ensures the optimum blood supply to various parts of the body. This helps in the flushing out of toxins from every nook and cranny as well as providing nourishment up to the last point. This leads to benefits such as delayed ageing, energy and a remarkable zest for life.

Excellent toning of the muscles

Muscles that have become flaccid, weak or slothy are stimulated repeatedly to shed excess flab and flaccidity.

But these enormous physical benefits are just a "side effect" of this powerful practice. What yoga does is harmonise the mind with the body and this result in real quantum benefits. It is now an open secret that the will of the

mind has enabled people to achieve extraordinary physical feats, which proves beyond doubt the mind and body connection.

Yoga through meditation works remarkably to achieve this harmony and helps the mind work in sync with the body. How often do we find that we are unable to perform our activities properly and in a satisfying manner because of the confusions and conflicts in our mind weigh down heavily upon us? Moreover, stress which in reality is the #1 killer affecting all parts of our physical, endocrinal and emotional systems can be corrected through the wonderful yoga practice of meditation.

In fact yoga = meditation, because both work together in achieving the common goal of unity of mind, body and spirit – a state of eternal bliss.

The meditative practices through yoga help in achieving an emotional balance through detachment. What it means is that meditation creates conditions, where you are not affected by the happenings around you. This in turn creates a remarkable calmness and a positive outlook, which also has tremendous benefits on the physical health of the body.

These are just some of the tangible benefits that can be achieved through yoga.

Having seen this, it is educative to note why the ancient yogis performed yoga and the interdependence of yoga and meditation. The ultimate goal of the yogis was "self-realisation" or "enlightenment", a concept, which perhaps is quite esoteric to you and me.

But what is interesting is that for this they had to meditate for extensive spells of time – days, weeks and much more. This required tremendous physical fitness, energy and the capacity to subsist on next to nothing. Yoga positions or asanas provided them the fullest fitness with the least metabolism or stress and meditation in turn provided them the strength and will to perform these asanas effectively – a virtuous cycle of cause and effect. This mutually symbiotic relationship helped them in their path.

Other benefits of yoga

- Brings down stress and enhances powers of relaxation
- Boosts physical strength, stamina and flexibility
- Bestows greater powers of concentration and self-control
- Inculcates impulse control
- Helps in rehabilitation of old and new injuries
- Intensifies tolerance to pain and enhancing mental clarity
- Boosts functioning of the immune system
- Enhances posture and muscle tone
- Improves blood circulation
- Results in healthy, glowing skin

- Cleanses and improves overall organ functioning
- Bestows peace of mind and a more positive outlook to life
- Infuses a sense of balance and internal harmony

Best of all, Yoga is highly therapeutic. Some of the ailments proven to be relieved, reversed and even healed through the practice of Yoga are acidity, allergies, alzheimer disease, anemia, anger, anxiety, arthritis, asthma, back pain, bronchitis, cancer, carpal tunnel syndrome, chronic fatigue, colitis, common cold, constipation, depression, diabetes, epilepsy, eye problems, facial wrinkles, gastro-intestinal disorders, headaches, heartburn, hemorrhoids, hepatitis, high blood pressure, hypertension, immune-deficiency, impotence, menopause, menstrual cramps, migraines, multiple sclerosis, muscular dystrophy, nervous tension, obesity, osteoporosis, prostate, enlargement, sciatica, skin problems, sleep apnea, slipped disk, sterility, stiffness, stress, insomnia, intoxication, thyroid problems, kidney stones, stuttering and stammering, urinary tract disorders for women, and many more.

Spiritual benefits of yoga

Yoga awakens a new consciousness. It makes one humble enough to do introspection. Consequently, there is an integration of personality.

Have a look at the lifetime spiritual benefits arising from regular yogic exercises:

1. Mental poise;
2. better awareness;
3. Unruffled serenity;
4. Mind turns inwards;
5. Inner peace is achieved;
6. Control over emotions;
7. Hallucinations disappear;
8. Increased control over mind;
9. Augmented concentration faculty;
10. Mind freed from the yoke of senses;
11. Baser instincts roped; Craving for the animal passions dies out;
12. Your deeds, thoughts and words become logical and meaningful.

■

The Concept of Karma

Karma is the concept of "action" or "deed" in Indian religions understood as that which causes the entire cycle of cause and effect *(samsara)* described in Hindu, Jain, Sikh and Buddhist philosophies.

Karma originated in the Vedic system of religion, otherwise known as Hinduism. As a term, it can at the latest be traced back to the early Upanishads, around 1500 BCE. In its major conception, karma is the physical, mental and supramental system of neutral rebound, "cause and effect" that is inherent in existence within the bounds of time, space, and causation. Essentially what this means is that the very being which one experiences on (as a human being) is governed by an immutable preservation of energy, vibe, and action.

Karma, for these reasons, naturally implies reincarnation or rebirth (though the opposite is not true) since thoughts and deeds in past lives will affect one's current situation. Thus, every individual alike is responsible for the tragedies and good 'fortunes' which are experienced. The concept of an inscrutable "God" figure is not necessary with the idea of karma. It is vital to note that karma is not an instrument of a god, or a single God, but is rather the physical and spiritual 'physics' of being. As gravity governs the motions of heavenly bodies and objects on the surface of the earth, karma governs the motions and happenings of life, both inanimate and animate, unconscious and conscious, in the cosmic realm.

Thus, what certain philosophical viewpoints may term "destiny" or "fate" is in actuality, according to believers of karma, the simple and neutral working out of karma. Many have likened karma to a moral banking system, a credit and debit of good and bad.

However, this view falls short of the idea that any sort of action (action being a root meaning of 'karma'), whether we term it 'good' or 'bad', binds us in recurring cause and effect. In order to attain supreme consciousness, to escape the cycle of life, death, and rebirth and the knot of karma one must altogether transcend karma. This method of transcendence is variously dealt with in many streams of not only Hinduism and Buddhism, but other faiths and philosophical systems as well.

From Hinduism the concept of karma was absorbed and developed in different manners in other movements within the other Indian religions of Buddhism, Jainism, and Sikhism. Although these religions express significant disagreement regarding the particularities of "karma", all four groups have relatively similar notions of what karma is. More recently the concept has been adopted (with various degrees of understanding) by many New Age movements, Theosophy and Kardecist Spiritualism.

The philosophical explanation of karma can differ slightly between traditions, but the general concept is basically the same. It is usually understood as a sum of all that an individual has done, is currently doing and will do. The results or 'fruits' of actions are called karma-phala. Karma is not about retribution, vengeance, punishment or reward; karma simply deals with what is. The effects of all deeds actively create past, present and future experiences, thus making one responsible for one's own life, and the pain and joy it brings to others. In religions that incorporate reincarnation, karma extends through one's present life and all past and future lives as well.

Throughout this process, some traditions (i.e., the Vedanta), believe that God plays some kind of role, for example, as the dispenser of the fruits of karma or as exercising the option to change one's karma in rare instances. In general, followers of Buddhism and many Hindus consider the natural laws of causation sufficient to explain the effects of karma. Another view holds that a Sadguru, acting on God's behalf, can mitigate or work out some of the karma of the disciple.

Law of Karma

All living creatures are responsible for their karma — their actions and the effects of their actions — and for their release from samsara. The concept can be traced back to the early Upanishads.

The esoteric Christian tradition, Essenian and later Rosicrucian schools teach it as the "Law of Cause and Consequence/Effect." However, this western esoteric tradition adds that the essence of the teachings of Christ is that the law of sin and death may be overcome by Love, which will restore immortality.

It is important to notice for example, that the views on karma adopted by the "modern" Christian faith or any other denomination promoting fear as a way to understand God, are difficult to understand. Karma is very simple to understand: an action brings a reaction.

At the same time, karma is also extremely intricate in it's application. This is neither good nor bad, it simply brings to the foreground the element of choice that we all have. Having a look at the daily news will bring an understanding of the laws of karma as they are plainly exhibited for all to see.

As spiritual beings, we presently experience in this world the reactions of our thinking process. Today's Christian faith embraces the: "you shall burn in hell eternally" model if one deviates from the prescribed "laws" of God. Well, there is a point to be made here. This "you shall burn in hell eternally" model was put in place to control people by means of fear and does not reflect in any way the teachings of Christ whatsoever. Love of God is developed through free will, never by fear. This world is simply and only but a karma laboratory meant to conduct the experience of reconnecting to love of God, and all of us, being a part and parcel of God, can do so by practicing with each other. The moment we can love, and love here is used in it's most profound meaning of the ultimate experience of giving and receiving unconditionally, then we have made use of the 'laboratory' in an efficient way. Karma is neither good or bad but rather an indicator to show us if the strategies we use to meet our needs are promoting life as a wonderful experience of not. Life itself is simple; we all share the same needs behind the cloak of 'modern' life. Karma is an ally to help us see how close we are to achieve our ultimate goal in this world; love.

Exceptions

Actions do not create karma (good or bad) when performed by an individual in the state of Moksha or liberation. Such a person is called "Stithaprajna". The monist, Adi Sankara taught "Akarmaiva Moksha," which means "Moksha can be attained only by doing, not by a process of effort". All actions performed by one in the state of Moksha are called Dharma.

Karma in the Hinduism

Karma came into being in Hinduism, based on the Vedas

and Upanishads. One of the first and most dramatic illustrations of Karma can be found in the great Hindu epic, the Mahabharata. The original Hindu concept of karma was later enhanced by several other movements within the religion, most notably Vedanta, Yoga, and Tantra.

Hinduism sees karma as immutable law with involuntary and voluntary acts being part of a more intricate system of cause and effect that is often not comprehensible to one bound by karma.

It is the goal of the Hindu, as expressed succinctly in the *Bhagavad Gita*, to embrace a 'sattvic' lifestyle and thus avoid creating more karma (karma is not qualified as good or bad). By ceasing to create more karma, the jiva-atma or individual soul is able to move closer to Moksha, or liberation.

To the Hindu, karma is the law of the phenomenal cosmos that is part and parcel of living within the dimensions of time and space. All actions, thoughts, vibrations of any sort, are governed by a law that demands perfect rebound. So all jiva-atmas (individual souls) must experience karma if they live and experience the phenomenal universe. To escape the cycle of life, death and rebirth, one must exhaust one's karma and realise one's true Self as the highest truth of Oneness that is Brahman (or for dvaitists (dualists) bliss with the Supreme Godhead). In Hinduism, karma is of three kinds:

Prarabadha Karma

This karma is unchangeable within the scope of one life, since it is the 'setup' for the life in question. It is the karma of one's past lives. After death, the atma leaves the body, as the casting off of old vestments, and carries with it the samskaras (impressions) of the past life of thoughts and actions and events. These samskaras manifest themselves in the unchangeable situation into which one is born and certain key events in one's life. These include one's time of death (seen as governed by an allotment from birth of the total number of one's breaths for that life), one's economic status, one's family (or lack of family), one's body type and look: essentially, the setting of one's birth, the initial base.

Samchita Karma

The samskaras that one inherits from the last lives create one's personality, inclinations, talents, the things that make up one's persona. One's likings, abilities, attitudes and inclinations are based on the thoughts and actions of past lives. One's samchita karma is somewhat alterable through practice and effort towards change. This might be seen through the Hindu system of Yoga and the dynamic of the gunas. An example would be someone who, through meditation, slowly evolved into a more stable personality.

Agami Karma

Agami karma is the karma of the present life over which the soul has complete control. Through it one creates one's karma in the present for the future of the current life and in life-times to come.

The Hindu cannot say, sometimes, if a major event in life is the doing of Prarabadha or Agami Karma. The idea of "bad things happening to good people" is seen by the Hindu as a result of Prarabadha Karma, more simply understood as karma from a past life.

In Hinduism, karma works within a cyclical framework that sees the phenomenal universe being created and eventually dissolving back into itself, back into realization that it was nothing other than Maya imposed on the truth of Brahman. So Karma will eventually be worked out.

Karma does allow for anirudh (Divine Grace). Through exceeding devotion and love of God, the Hindu believes one can be helped to speed through Karma phal (Karmic fruit). By developing 'vairagya' or 'detachment' from the fruits of one's karma, as Lord Krishna most famously summarised, one can transcend karma and be liberated. One is aided by love of God. All the Yogas of Hinduism seek to transcend karma through different means of realisation.

Karma in Buddhism

In Buddhism, only intentional actions are karmic "acts of will". The 'Law of Karma' refers to "cause and effect", but Karma literally means "action" – often indicating intent or cause. Accompanying this usually is a separate tenet called Vipaka, meaning result or effect. The re-action or effect can itself also influence an action, and in this way, the chain of causation continues ad infinitum.

When Buddhists talk about karma, they are normally referring to karma/action that is 'tainted' with ignorance - karma that continues to ensure that the being remains in the everlasting cycle of samsara.

This samsaric karma comes in two 'flavours' – 'good' karma, which leads to positive/pleasurable experiences, like high rebirth (as a deva, asura, or human), and bad karma which leads to suffering and low rebirth (as a hell-sufferer, as a preta, or as an animal). There is also a completely different type of karma that is neither good nor bad, but liberating. This karma allows for the individual to break the uncontrolled cycle of rebirth which always implies suffering, and thereby leave samsara to permanently enter Nirvana.

The Buddhist sutras explain that in order to generate liberating karma, we must first develop incredibly powerful concentration, and proper insight into the (un)reality of samsara. This concentration is akin to the states of mind required to be reborn in the Deva realm, and in itself depends upon a very deep training in ethical self-discipline.

This differentiation between good karma and liberating karma has been used by some scholars to argue that the development of Tantra depended upon Buddhist ideas and philosophies. Understanding the universal law of Karma provides order to a beginningless and endless universe. Alongside this view is the related notion of Buddhist rebirth – sometimes understood to be the same thing as reincarnation – which has its roots in the principle of Karma.

Karma is one of those words we don't translate. Its basic meaning is simple enough — action — but because of the weight the Buddha's teachings give to the role of action, the Sanskrit word karma packs in so many implications that the English word action can't carry all its luggage. This is why we've simply airlifted the original word into our vocabulary.

But when we try unpacking the connotations the word carries now that it has arrived in everyday usage, we find that most of its luggage has gotten mixed up in transit. In the eyes of most Americans, karma functions like fate — bad fate, at that: an inexplicable, unchangeable force coming out of our past, for which we are somehow vaguely responsible and powerless to fight. "I guess it's just my karma," I've heard people sigh when bad fortune strikes with such force that they see no alternative to resigned acceptance.

The fatalism implicit in this statement is one reason why so many of us are repelled by the concept of karma, for it sounds like the kind of callous myth-making that can justify almost any kind of suffering or injustice in the status quo: "If he's poor, it's because of his karma." From this it seems a short step to saying that he or she deserves to suffer, and so doesn't deserve our help.

This misperception comes from the fact that the Buddhist concept of karma came to the West at the same time as non-Buddhist concepts, and so ended up with some of their luggage.

Although many Asian concepts of karma are fatalistic, the early Buddhist concept was not fatalistic at all. In fact, if we look closely at early Buddhist ideas of karma, we'll find that they give even less importance to myths about the past than most modern people do.

For the early Buddhists, karma was non-linear and complex. Other Indian schools believed that karma operated in a simple straight line, with actions from the past influencing the present, and present actions influencing the future.

As a result, they saw little room for free will. Buddhists, however, saw that karma acts in multiple feedback loops, with the present moment being shaped both by past and by present actions; present actions shape not only the future but also the present. Furthermore, present actions need not be determined by past actions. In other words, there is free will, although its range is somewhat dictated by the past. The nature of this freedom is symbolized in an image used by the early Buddhists: flowing water. Sometimes the flow from the past is so strong that little can be done except to stand fast, but there are also times when the flow is gentle enough to be diverted in almost any direction.

So, instead of promoting resigned powerlessness, the early Buddhist notion of karma focused on the liberating potential of what the mind is doing with every moment. Who you are — what you come from — is not anywhere near as important as the mind's motives for what it is doing right now.

Even though the past may account for many of the inequalities we see in life, our measure as human beings is not the hand we've been dealt, for that hand can change at any moment. We take our own measure by how well we play the hand we've got. If you're suffering, you try not to continue the unskillful mental habits that would keep that particular karmic feedback going. If you see that other people are suffering, and you're in a position to help, you focus not on their karmic past but your karmic opportunity in the present: Someday you may find yourself in the same predicament that they're in now, so here's your opportunity to act in the way you'd like them to act toward you when that day comes.

This belief that one's dignity is measured, not by one's past, but by one's present actions, flew right in the face of the Indian traditions of caste-based hierarchies, and explains why early Buddhists had such a field day poking fun at the pretensions and mythology of the brahmans. As the Buddha pointed out, a brahman could be a superior person not because he came out of a brahman womb, but only if he acted with truly skillful intentions.

We read the early Buddhist attacks on the caste system, and aside from their anti-racist implications, they often strike us as quaint. What we fail to realise is that they strike right at the heart of our myths about our own past: our obsession with defining who we are in terms of where we come from — our race, ethnic heritage, gender, socio-economic background, sexual preference — our modern tribes. We put inordinate amounts of energy into creating and maintaining the mythology of our tribe so that we can take vicarious pride in our tribe's good name. Even when we become Buddhists, the tribe comes first. We demand a Buddhism that honors our myths.

From the standpoint of karma, though, where we come from is old karma, over which we have no control. What we "are" is a nebulous concept at best — and pernicious at worst, when we use it to find excuses for acting on unskilful motives. The worth of a tribe lies only in the skilful actions of its individual members. Even when those good people belong to our tribe, their good karma is theirs, not ours. And, of course, every tribe has its bad members, which means that the mythology of the tribe is a fragile thing. To hang onto anything fragile requires a large investment of passion, aversion, and delusion, leading inevitably to more unskilful actions on into the future.

So the Buddhist teachings on karma, far from being a

quaint relic from the past, are a direct challenge to a basic thrust — and basic flaw — in our culture. Only when we abandon our obsession with finding vicarious pride in our tribal past, and can take actual pride in the motives that underlie our present actions, can we say that the word karma, in its Buddhist sense, has recovered its luggage. And when we open the luggage, we'll find that it's brought us a gift: the gift we give ourselves and one another when we drop our myths about who we are, and can instead be honest about what we're doing with each moment — at the same time making the effort to do it right.

■

Religious thoughts for Successful Living

Religion and Well-being

According to a recent study, faith-based positive religious resources can protect psychological well-being through enhanced hope and perceived social support during stressful experiences, like undergoing cardiac surgery. Furthermore, having negative religious thoughts and struggles may hinder recovery.

Although the connection between religiosity and health-related well-being has been studied for years, recent research found that the connection between religion and well-being is more complex than past studies suggested. The researchers found that perceived social support and hope contributed to less depression and anxiety for post-operative patients who used positive religious coping styles in their every day lives.

The contribution of social support to hope suggests that those who perceive more support at this critical moment may feel more hopeful about their recovery.

Acts of positive religious coping include religious forgiveness, seeking spiritual support, collaborative religious coping, spiritual connection, religious purification and thoughts of religious benevolence.

Negative coping styles are associated with the inability of patients to protect their psychological well-being against the distress of depression and anxiety that tend to predict poor post-operative recovery in the literature.

This relationship is related to poor mental health at both preoperative and post-operative times, indicating ongoing faith-based struggles.

Negative coping patterns consist of spiritual discontent, thoughts of punishing God, insecurity, demonic thoughts, interpersonal religious discontent, religious doubt, and discontented spiritual relations.

These pathways appear to be key in understanding how religious coping styles may be helpful or harmful to a person's ability to handle stressful situations. These findings imply that health and mental health professionals should be more attentive to faith factors as inspirational or motivational springboards in some contexts.

Hinduism: Living the Religious Life

The Hindu religion is an ocean of spiritual teachings about all aspects of life and consciousness. It's the world's oldest religion, going back to the very dawn of history. It sees its origin in the cosmic mind itself.

Yet Hinduism is also perhaps the world's youngest religion because it emphasises the authority of living teachers and allows for correction and evolution over time.

Hinduism is the most diverse religious tradition in the world. It could be said that there are probably more religions inside of Hinduism than outside of it. It has numerous saints, sages, and yogis, both male and female, from ancient to modern times, and today still has what is probably the largest number of monks and renunciates (including a number of Westerners). The recent Hindu religious gathering, the Kumbha Mela of January 2001, had tens of millions of people in attendance. It was the largest gathering of any type and the largest religious gathering in the history of the world.

Hinduism is the world's largest non-biblical tradition, with nearly a billion followers worldwide. It could be called the world's largest non-organised religion as it emphasises individual spiritual experience, the realisation of the higher Self over any religious institution, book, dogma, or savior.

It's also the world's largest native or pagan tradition, reflecting the ancient spiritual traditions that once existed all over the world. Like native traditions everywhere, it honors God or the sacred throughout all nature. It has many insights in harmony with the ecological age, as it affords reverence to the Earth as a conscious and loving presence and asks us to respect our environment.

Hinduism contains the world's oldest and largest tradition of Goddess worship– worshipping the Divine not only as father but also as mother. It recognises all the diverse forms of the Goddess and her powers of wisdom, beauty, strength, love, and compassion.

Perhaps most notably, Hinduism is the world's largest pluralistic tradition, recognising One Truth– an eternal reality of Being-Consciousness Bliss in all beings– but also many paths to realise it. Hinduism recognises theism (the belief in One Creator) but only as one portion of the human religious experience that includes polytheism, pantheism, monism, and even atheism.

As the most inclusive of the world's great religions, Hinduism has room for all these views and yet guides us through these to Self-realisation that transcends them all.

Hinduism has probably the world's oldest and largest literature of spirituality, mysticism, and yoga. It provides a complete spiritual culture including art, dance, sculpture, medicine, and science, with all these subjects explained according to a science of consciousness.

The Four Goals of Life

Classic Hinduism promotes four different goals. Like other aspects of Hinduism, the goals are split between those emphasised by the "life is good" perspective and those emphasised by the "life is bad" perspective. The three life-affirming goals are *Dharma* (virtue), *Artha* (success) and *Kama* (pleasure), while the life-negating goal is that of moksha (release).

The three "life is good" goals can be pursued all at once or at different times in one's life. Some goals seem more suited to different stages of life than others.

Dharma is the practice of virtue, the living of an ethical and ritually correct life. The definition of what is virtuous, however, varies, depending on a person's caste and *jati* membership. The primary virtue is to fulfil the duties assigned to one's caste. Thus a Brahmin should offer sacrifices and do them to the best of his ability, while a Vaishya silversmith should create his plates and bowls as strong and beautiful as possible. If either person tried to do the other's job, that would be seen as violating their caste duty. The dharma a person is expected to fulfil also varies depending on their stage of life. A student, for instance, becomes virtuous through a different set of actions than a householder.

Artha is the working for and achieving of success, in terms of both wealth and power. This means it is religiously important to be a successful businessman, to sell a lot of carpets for instance, or to manage a successful restaurant. It also means that it is religiously good to serve on the city council, to be active in civic organisations, or even to become a politician. This kind of success is most easily achieved at the householder stage of life.

Kama is pleasure, usually understood as aesthetic pleasure of all kinds. This includes: the producing and enjoyment of art, music, dance, drama, literature, poetry, and sex. (The "Kama Sutra," which may be one of the best known Hindu texts in the West, is about the aesthetic pleasure of men and women; it discusses beauty, music, dance and sexual activity.)

It is thus religiously praiseworthy to take part, to support, or just to appreciate any form of pleasure. This should always be done, of course, within the realm of dharma (i.e., in a virtuous manner).

The "life is bad" goal is moksha. It is the striving for release from life (since, after all, it is bad). To achieve this, a person must turn their back on life and strive to live without the things that make up life.

At first, it requires the turning away from the first three goals, of rejecting family, comforts, pleasure, education, and so on. It also requires one to become an ascetic, a hermit, and to spend one's time in contemplation.

This contemplation should be directed towards overcoming the *maya* that clouds human perception of reality and towards realising the true nature of the cosmos and one's place in it (that Atman and Brahman are one).

Hinduism: A Way of Successful Life

There is a misconception among many Hindus that since Hinduism is not a religion in the strictest sense of the word, but a way of life, everything that we do in life is acceptable to the religion.

Hinduism does indicate that every individual is completely responsible for his actions and the way he leads his life. It gives complete freedom to the individual to follow his inner nature and explore his inner world in order to arrive at Truth.

But this does not mean that it advocates permissiveness or incorrect way of life. It cautions one to be wary of the illusory nature of life and suggests several ways and means to deal with it.

The scriptures make it amply clear that whoever indulges in wrong actions has to suffer from the consequences. The epics and the stories from the Puranas convincingly illustrate this fact. They depict how the *asuras* or demons leading their lives wrongly and egoistically and indulging in incorrect actions suffered from divine retribution.

Again and again they emphasise in many words, aphorisms, stories and verses how wrong actions would lead one towards the darker worlds and one own downfall.

The religious freedom it offers therefore should not be misconstrued as religious permissiveness. A person who chooses a wrong way of life has to suffer from the consequences of his own actions. Religious freedom means to live life with a great sense of responsibility, not irresponsibility. The responsibility is primarily and essentially towards maintaining and following ones basic dharma.

Hinduism does emphasise that one should lead ones life in accordance with ones dharma and the scriptures. Those who try to rationalise their wrong actions and incorrect living do so at their own peril. In this regard there is neither confusion nor contradiction as to what the religion stands and what it upholds. Let us examine how true this is.

According to Hinduism an individual has to live in order to observe and protect his dharma or religious laws. If he does not observe his dharma, he is not entitled to moksha or salvation.

An individual must be ever grateful to his gods who always keep a protective eye over him and work for his welfare. If he does not propitiate them or acknowledge their help, he will lose their support and blessings. These gods exists not only outside of him, but also within him. They are the spiritual energies that reside in him and help him to progress towards Aditi, the Light and attain "Soma", the state of divine bliss.

It does not mean that the gods are selfish or biased. It means that the gods are impartial, as they discharge their respective duties strictly in accordance with the rules of creation and the Eternal Dharma, laid down by the Supreme Self, rewarding righteous actions and punishing the unrighteous ones.

The scriptures are very clear as to what should be ones attitude towards the religious texts. An individual must revere and respect the Vedas which are revealed texts directly coming from God for the general welfare and guidance of the mankind. The attitude that is expected of a devout Hindu should include, respect towards the sacred books, proper study and understanding of them and proper observation of the truths and laws prescribed there in.

An individual must learn to see the omnipresence of God in every thing and everywhere. He who sees Him in all and all in Him would lead a deeply religious and spiritual life, because having realised the presence of God in all, he develops compassion and right attitude towards the whole creation of God.

An individual must lead life in strict accordance with the laws laid down in the scriptures. He must perform daily rituals, various samskaras and live the four ashramas or stages of his life in accordance with the rules prescribed in the scriptures.

It is unfortunate that many modern Hindus have a great contempt for the observation of rituals which according to them are nothing short of superstition. It must be remembered that these rituals are meant to inculcate feelings of reverence and devotion to god or gods.

A ritual is a method or a way. When we speak of the fact that Hinduism is a way of life, we are actually saying that one should live life as if it is a sacred ritual. The whole process of living is a great ritual in which the individual offers himself as a sacrificial offering to the divine spark within him and reaches the highest state of realisation.

Let us not forget that spiritualism is also a kind of ritualism only in which the spirit follows a certain prescribed path and reaches its original state. The emphasis on rituals in the Vedas is suggestive of the fact that we are expected to lead our lives according to a way or a method that would ensure our salvation.

It is not an exaggeration to say that some degree of ritualism is essential and integral to every religion. Whether it is religion or military activity, management or holding a meeting, rituals add structure and discipline to ones activity.

However superfluous they may appear to be, rituals prepare us mentally for the occasion. They divert the attention of an otherwise busy individual from mundane activities and make him god-centred. It does not mean that one should follow the rituals blindly. One has the freedom to chose the rituals which according to him would ensure proper results.

One can always create or formulate one's own rituals as long as they incorporate the original meaning and serve the same purpose for which they are originally meant. One can at the most discard a few of those rituals which offend ones own sense of justice or balance.

But it is doubtful if the religion would condone those who would discard all rituals summarily, without proper understanding of what the rituals stand for.

One need not perform a *yagna* in the elaborate manner prescribed in the Vedas, especially when one is not conversant with Sanskrit or the vedic ritualism. One need not perform even puja if one has the right awareness and correct attitude towards God and oneself.

If one understands the true meaning of a *yagna* and try to make an offering of something mentally with sincerity and devotion it will lead to the same results. If one can close ones eyes in front of the image of a god and mentally performs a puja with sincerity and devotion, it would lead to the same results as the physical puja performed with the same degree of devotion and sincerity.

What is important is the attitude and feeling behind performing the act, not the mere act itself. The Upanishads at various places cautions the students against insincere and empty ritualism.

Many Hindus of modern day have a poor understanding of the religious scriptures. Some very educated Hindus cannot even recollect with accuracy the names of the four Vedas. Some of them do not have an idea of what the Upanishads teach.

But they try to justify their religious fervor under the feeling that such knowledge is neither essential nor useful for ones spiritual progress.

Hinduism may be just a way of life, and not religion. But it does not under any circumstances advocates one to be irreligious or irresponsible towards oneself. It always emphasises on the need to protect ones Dharma and follow ones natural Dharma. Your dharma is not something that is imposed upon you. It is something that you are born with. It is a part of your previous samskaras. You cannot just wish it away.

And no society can impose its code upon you. If you are born with a particular sense of dharma and your society tries to manipulate you with its own codes you have the right and freedom to chose your own code. This is where the religion gives freedom to the individual to select his path. This is where it tries to act as a buffer between the individual and the conditioning and controlling influence of an all powerful society.

The original vedic texts never prescribed rigid social structure. They only suggested that one should live in accordance with the laws of dharma and ones own inner nature. The nature of man is understandably imperfect and unless he brings it in harmony with the laws of dharma, he cannot make spiritual progress.

The word "dharma" has a very comprehensive meaning in Hinduism. Dharma means the Eternal Law, the Law of God. It is also all those factors that arise out of it or lead ones towards it. It means religion, ones beliefs and faith, justice, righteousness, performing morally acceptable actions, being on the positive side of life. It also means the universal order, ones own inner nature, ones duty and responsibility towards oneself and towards others.

Hinduism never says that if ones dharma is attacked one should let it go and let the dharma be destroyed. Even God would not sit quite if there is an ascendance of adharma in the society. He would incarnate in order to restore dharma and destroy evil or adharma. The texts are very clear in this regard.

Life is a battle-field in which there is a fierce battle and competition between the good (dharma) and bad (adharma) forces. The same battle goes on in ones physical body and mind. It is a part of ones dharma to protect and guard oneself against external and harmful influences which lead to ones inner imbalance and destruction of ones moral character.

The modern day Hindus, not all but a sizeable number of them, do not read the sacred texts because of lack of proper attitude and faith. They do not see any perceptible use in the exercise of reading. They take comfort in the misguided belief that the texts are ritualistic in nature and therefore it would not make any sense to read them or follow them.

They believe that one need not read these texts, one need not understand them, one need not even believe in God, but still can work for their salvation! How absurd the belief can be! How difficult it would be to attain Him with such a high degree of insincerity, self-deception and rationalisation of knowledge!

The Vedas are not texts of empty eulogy and ritualism, extolling the virtues of gods and goddesses who appear more like human beings with the same number of defects as we find in ourselves. The texts are impregnated with tremendous degree of divine wisdom. They reveal innumerable secrets to those who have the interest like Shri Aurobindo to unravel the hidden key and try to understand their true meaning. Those who have any doubts in this regard should read his book, *the Secret of the Vedas* to understand what the Vedic texts actually means.

Many Hindu texts are presently available at reasonable prices all over the world from many sources. One does not lose any thing by going through these books and trying to understand what they actually mean. These books definitely help one to gain an insight into the basics of

Hindu religion and help one to develop a correct attitude towards ones religion. At least we will be able to know correctly what is the right way of living.

Let us remember that in other religions, scriptures do occupy the central part. These religions are more organised because an understanding of the basic scripture is fundamental to the practice of religion. While there are hundreds of Hindus who have never read a Veda or Upanishads, it is difficult to come across a Christian or a Muslim who has never gone through his or her holy book. Many carry them to their places of work or keep it in their houses for regular or occasional study. It is wrong to presume that Hinduism does not prescribe study of religious scriptures. In fact it is an essential and integral part of a person's education and religious life.

An individual has freedom in Hinduism to chose what is right for him or her, but only after careful examination and analysis of a given situation. One can always use ones *buddhi* or intelligence to know what is right and appropriate in any given situation, without rationalising ones inactivity, lack of interest and indifference.

Let us remember that Hinduism does not prescribe any way of life, but a way of life in accordance with ones Dharma as prescribed in the religious texts, especially the Vedas and the other sacred literature. One should also have a clear idea of what is superstition and obscurantism, in order to make his way of life, the correct way of life. But one should never dismiss the very reading of the literature as an exercise in futility. That would amount to leading a way of life like a blind man groping in the darkness and accepting his blindness as way of life.

Swami Vivekanand once remarked about Hinduism that the Hindu man drinks religiously, sleeps religiously, walks religiously, marries religiously.

Hinduism is not considered to be a religion but a way of life, because religion is deeply interwoven into the life of a Hindu the way nerves are interwoven in our bodies. It is very difficult to separate living and religion in the life of a devout Hindu. Both are inseparable. Both compliment each other. Both exist because of each other and both would lose their meaning and significance without the other. Religion is the centre of living and living is the centre of religion.

Here we will try to understand the philosophy hidden behind this beautiful and noble concept of life and why a Hindu considers his it as a way of life rather than as a religion.

Religion is there in every aspect of a Hindu's life. Religion is his inseparable companion, guide and philosopher. It is there, always, however modern or advanced he may be, whether he believes in God or not, at the back of his mind, like a tuft of hair on the head of a priest, deeply rooted in his subconscious, firmly entrenched in his being, from which he cannot escape even if he chooses to follow another religion.

It is there when he is born, as if he comes into this world carrying with him the burden of his religion, with all his deeply rooted religious beliefs and practices, as if they are his traditional family tools from which he can never be separated, because his present life is but a continuation and result of his past one.

And it stays with him till the end, influencing every action of his and helping him to adjust to the harsh realities of life in a rather philosophical and stoical way and accept suffering as a part of his self-purification and inner correction.

According to Hinduism, religion is not separate from living. It is living itself. God does not exist in temples and sacred places only. Going to the temples is a good practice, but that is not the only way to worship God. God does not exist in temples alone, in some particular altar or sacred place.

He exists every where and can be approached in every way, not just by performing some special *yagnas* and rituals, but also through the very process of living ones life and discharging ones responsibility towards oneself, ones family, ones society and ones own religion. Even helping other religions is not an abominable act.

The very life that we live on earth is divine. Every aspect of it is infused with Divine presence. Hidden behind the illusion of life is God's golden and immortal presence. If we are clever enough and careful enough in our thoughts and deeds, we can see His foot prints every where, in our lives and actions.

We can realise Him right amidst our active living process. If we are careful, if we are intelligent, if we have the right discrimination, we can make the very process of living a kind of daily worship, a means to establish contact with the Divine, a way to purify ourselves and ennoble ourselves, and create, in this very life, amidst this very society, a strong foundation, a lasting basis, for our spiritual growth that would eventually lead us towards self-realisation.

The Hindu way of life encourages us to accept living as a means of self-realisation. Every activity that we perform while living and every aspect of life that we know and deal with becomes means to realise God. In this approach there is very little difference between living and worshipping.

Life is but divine and sacred. The Divine does not exist elsewhere in some heavenly regions, separate and distinct from ours. He is right here, amidst us, at the centers of our very lives and activities. Every act that we perform in this life will either contribute towards our evolution or inhibit it.

Life is verily an opportunity to receive into our selves, the Divine force, the illuminating and enlightening awareness of God, the overwhelming and all encompassing should consciousness. Life is an opportunity to discover our hidden selves. It is a great way to go beyond our limited vision and limited capacities. It is the best possible instrument within our reach to realise Truth of ourselves and of God in the truest and grandest possible manner.

Performing ones duties with a sense of detachment and as an offering to God, or worshipping God in a temple or during a ritual, are conceptually one and the same. Self-realisation can be achieved not only by renouncing the world and performing *tapas*, but living amidst society, with a sense of detachment, untouched by the corruptions of life, like a lotus leaf in a pond.

If we live with a divine sense of responsibility, every act that we perform in the course of our lives can lead us into the mysteries of divine life and into highest transcendental state of light and delight.

Every Hindu artist brought in the true traditions of Hinduism know this secret. For him his art is simply an inseparable from of divine worship. For him it is the best and the easiest way to be in touch with the heart of God. His devotion to God flows out of him in the form of an artistic expression. His art flourishes to the extent he is devoted to God. It is the same conviction, the same philosophy, the same approach, which prompts a karmayogi to perform his duties with a degree of detachment that is rare to come across elsewhere in the world.

The present life is but a continuation of the previous. It is another opportunity that we create for ourselves to continue our experiments with truth, to correct our past mistakes, cleanse our souls and make ourselves more qualified for the infusion of light and ascent into higher planes of existence. The present is so because of the deeds of the past.

We are the creators of our own lives and destinies. We create them out of our right and wrong actions which have both positive and negative consequences. So if one has to change the conditions and secure a better future one has to live more responsibly and more carefully.

And this has to be done right now, here and in this very life. This is the philosophy, the line of thinking, behind the concept of Hinduism as a way of life. The concepts of the omnipresence of God and his inviolable law of life (dharma) operating universally keep the typical Hindu careful in his actions and responsible towards his own life. For the typical Hindu religion is thus a way of life, a means of self-purification and inner evolution.

■

5

Harmonise Yourself with Life

We create our reality through our perceptions and our way of being. The longer we live, the more we realise the impact of attitude on life. Attitude is more important than facts. It is more important than the past, than education, than money, than circumstances, than failures, than success, than what other people think or say or do. It is more important than appearance, gift, or skill. It will make or break a company, a church, a home.

The remarkable thing is we have a choice every day regarding the attitude we will embrace for that day. We cannot change our past, we cannot change the fact that people will act in a certain way. We cannot change the inevitable.

The only thing we can do is play on the string we have, and that is our attitude. Life is 10 per cent what happens to us and 90 per cent how we react to it.

Life is a Mirror

Yes, your entire life is a mirror of what is going on in your consciousness. It is a reflection of yourself. Each person, each event may be considered as a tool which can help you to know yourself better and better.

If you had a mirror which could perfectly reflect all that was inside of you, what would you see? Would you see a beautiful, magnificent world in the mirror, or would things look pretty much the same as they do right now?

To a large degree, the world around you is a mirror of that which is within you. You see what you look for. People treat you as you expect to be treated. The things you experience come from the actions you take.

Think of the world as a mirror of you, and consider whether or not you like what you see. More importantly, realise that you have the power to change it. Your world is a part of you. It is an expression of you. With your thoughts and actions, you can make it what you want it to be.

The Will to Harmonise

There are many conflicting forces which can be brought into harmony under this Will. One set of opposing forces that can be brought into harmony is energy that brings a love of ease and pleasure, a dislike of causing pain, procrastination, a desire to let things be, to rest, and to have no thought of consequences. The opposing energy is a fiery, impatient, ever-urging to action energy. These contrasting forces can make life one of continual warfare and unrest until these two forces are harmonised. Some people experience this as "driving with the brake on" while others may swing back and forth from expressing one aspect of this to the other. As you work with the Will to Harmonise, you can find a balance between action and inaction, between putting things off and getting them done, in just the right timing. Call upon this Will anytime you are feeling in conflict between opposing forces, such as wanting/ not wanting to move forward in some area of your life.

This Will awakens our intuition, which shows us the way of harmony and unity. Intuition comes spontaneously through our thoughts and feelings and tells us what actions to take to align with the Divine plan of our lives, with all the parts of ourselves, and with others. It is through listening to and using our intuition that we can know how to harmonise with the greater whole of life, release conflict, and experience the peace and love of our soul.

This is the Will that harmonises all the parts of your being, and that can assist you in taking your intuitive insights and feelings and in applying them appropriately to your life to create more harmony and beauty. Call upon the Will to Harmonise anytime you want to deepen your intuition, release conflict, and experience peace.

This is the illumined Will and is connected with the creation of art, music, and beauty in all forms. The Will to Harmony sees disharmony as ugliness, and Wills beauty to come about through creating harmonious relationships between all the parts. Sometimes this beauty will be expressed in form, color, and sound, such as through the creation of art and music. Sometimes this beauty will be expressed through the harmonizing of the higher self with the personality self, or harmonising with others, creating beauty in relationships.

As you play with this quality of Will, you may notice a greater appreciation or awareness of colour and sound. It is said that the universe is created of sound and colour. This Will carries the music of the spheres and you can experience it more through listening to beautiful, inspiring music. You can also experience this Will through looking at beauty, and through seeing beauty in all of its forms and expressions wherever you look. You can call upon the Will to Harmonise anytime you want to create beauty, in your emotions, body, thoughts, and through your creations such as books, music, art, dance, and anything you want to infuse with beauty.

Part of the role of humanity is to harmonise the higher kingdoms with the lower kingdoms of nature, acting as a channel for divine energy from the higher to the lower. By doing this humanity will bring about unity, harmony, and beauty in nature, and will harmonise humanity's souls with the souls of all life.

Some qualities of the Will to Harmonise: Power to penetrate the depths of matter, to reveal the path, to express divinity, and to create true beauty and the harmony of the spheres.

You can use the transformative energy of the Great One who is transmitting the Will to Harmonise. This Great Life is known by other names, such as the Ray of Harmony through Conflict, the Lord of Harmony, Beauty, and Art, the Great Revealer, the Divine Intermediary. Reflecting on these names can reveal much about the energy that this Great Life embodies and transmits to humanity.

The Will to Harmonise is in the middle of the seven Divine Wills and the planes of consciousness they link you with. There are three qualities of Divine Will that are higher, i.e., closer to the realms of pure God-Consciousness (The Will to Initiate, the Will to Unify, and the Will to Evolve) and there are three that are lower, i.e., closer to the physical world (the Will to Cause, the Will to Act, and the Will to Express).

Because it is a bridge between the lower and higher worlds, you can connect with the Will to Harmonise to "travel upward" and align with the higher forces in the universe. Although you can make this alignment without the Will to Harmonise, working with it assists you in coming into more complete alignment and harmony with the higher energies you get in touch with.

This Will harmonises the initial conflict that happens when two dissimilar energies, of different vibrations, qualities and frequencies, make contact. It allows them to come together in harmony, such as the energies of your personality and the energies of your soul.

The Will to Harmosize links you with the higher worlds and allows you to expand your consciousness in every possible way through identification with them. It can facilitate your being in harmony with the Divine Plan of the Universe, with the Masters, Enlightened Ones, Angels, and God/Goddess/All-That-Is. You can call in the power of the Will to Harmonise to strengthen your ability to harmonise the energy of your personality with your soul and align with the Divine Plan for your life. You can use the energy of the Will to Harmonise as a bridge linking you with all that is light and good within you, helping you to experience God-Consciousness.

The Will to Harmonise can reveal aspects of your highest path. It reveals the formless, subtle worlds of energy that are the cause and guiding force behind all outer events. It helps you harmonize with the Divine blueprint of your life and bring that Blueprint into the physical world.

The Will to Harmonise is a bridge that brings energies from the higher dimensions into the physical world. Its energy of wholeness and harmony can reach into the densest levels of matter, helping all life at every level of evolution to expand in consciousness and to realise their divinity and beauty.

The Will to Harmonise is a force of beauty, harmony, unity, and balance. It opens the possibility for all outer forms and happenings to be infused with the beauty of the higher, subtle worlds. You can call upon this Will to help you create harmony and beauty in all areas of your life, including creating beautiful emotions of calm and peace, a balanced life, art, music, and literature, a harmonious, beautiful environment, and anything else you want to infuse with beauty, harmony, balance, and unity.

The Will to Harmonise helps you stay on your higher path by releasing limitations. It releases the limitations and conflict you can experience by living in the physical world, a world of polarities. It helps you balance between, and then transcend the pairs of opposites. Being pulled between the pairs of opposites is a source of much conflict. When you go toward anything, you also encounter its opposite, seen as an opposing force. This opposing force is usually viewed as the limitation, the battlefield, and the source of conflict.

You can work with the Will to Harmonise to find balance as you walk on the "razor's edge" between the pairs of opposites. You can learn to go towards those things you want to create and minimise the impact of the opposing forces. You can stay in the centre of your being, moving forward, rather than being caught swinging back and forth between the opposing forces.

The Will to Harmonise has the ability to blend and harmonise higher and lower energies, so that which is lower and closer to form (such as your personality) does not resist the higher energies it can contact. It helps harmonise your personality desires with your soul's desires. Its energy helps release the limitations that form and substance (your mind, emotions, body, and matter itself) put upon your innermost self, your soul and spirit. Your personality becomes increasingly infused with the love, light, wisdom, creativity, power, will, and the higher intelligence of your soul. Your personality gains new power to live as your soul, and to carry out the Divine Plan of your life.

You can evoke the Will to Harmonise to strengthen all forms of intuition. Your intuition is your ability to sense and know a greater truth that is often veiled by the outer appearance of things. Intuition tells you what actions to take to bring the greatest good into your life. The Will to Harmonise can enhance spiritual intuition, where you intuitively know and sense your oneness with others and all life.

It can enhance your mental intuition, your ability to receive breakthrough ideas and new insights that come in a flash, or in a moment of "ah ha!" where you suddenly know what to do. Intuition can also come through your feelings or a physical, body sense.

It is through listening to and using your intuition that you can know how to harmonise with the greater whole of life, release conflict, and experience the peace and love of your soul. As humanity comes more completely under the influence of this Ray, intuitional awareness will become the norm and there will be oneness, love, and harmony.

The influence of this Will is beginning to touch humanity once again, and will be in its full flower throughout the next 600 years. Its influence will bring all manifested life into harmony with Spirit through harmonising the higher aspects of the Self with the personality. This alignment will allow many people to make great and rapid spiritual advancement. There will be a corresponding rapid adjustment in human affairs, particularly in connecting with and manifesting Divine Will.

The first three qualifies of Divine Will you have called upon — the Will to Initiate, the Will to Unify, and the Will to Evolve — are considered the three major rays. The qualities of the Will to Harmonise as well as the next three Rays: the Will to Act, the Will to Cause, and the Will to Express, are considered aspects of the first three major rays, and merge in the third ray, the Will to Evolve.

The qualities of the Fourth, Fifth, Sixth and Seventh Wills bring through more of the energies and purposes of the first three aspects of Divine Will. There are other Great Ones holding additional qualities of Divine Will that are not active at this time, but are awaiting the proper time and period to become influential over the next thousand years.

Contacting the Will to Harmonise

Use the process that follows to contact the Will to
Harmonise, taking another step on your path of spiritual
growth.

1. Relax your body, and breathe in a relaxed way.

2. Prepare to receive the Will to Harmonise by asking:
   Am I willing to release limitation? Am I ready to
   live a beautiful life, in harmony with all beings? Am
   I willing to let go of the battles and struggle, and to
   find peace and an end to conflict in my life? Am I
   ready to strengthen, recognise, and act upon my
   intuition?

3. If you feel ready, call upon and blend with your soul,
   feeling its loving presence.

4. Using your imagination, sense the souls of others
   who are connecting with the Great Ones transmitting
   Divine Will. If you would like, join with the group
   call to the Great One who transmits the Will to
   Harmonise. Joining with others at the soul level,
   who are also calling upon Divine Will, can assist you
   in receiving more of the full spectrum of the energy
   that is sent in response to your call for it.

5. The Great Life who embodies the Will to Harmonise
   always responds to your call, and does so now.

6. A ray of light, like a beam of sunlight, is sent to you.
   Receive the energy of the Will to Harmonize into
   your heart centre, an energy centre located

around the area of your physical heart. This awakens your ability to stay balanced and centred in your heart, aligned with your soul and the higher realms of light, beyond the pull of the opposing forces.

7.   Allow the energy of the Will to Harmonise to touch and transform you. Invite it into your life, and open to receive all the gifts of consciousness it has for you.

8.   Feel the love and harmony that is available to you as you link with the Will to Harmonise. Practice calling upon and experiencing the energy of the Will to Harmonise often. Call upon this Great One and receive Its transmission of harmony and love into your heart centre any time you want to feel more harmonious, be in harmony with another person, your soul, if you are in a conflict you want to resolve; to draw in music, colour, sound; or to bring beauty to anything and to any area of your life you choose.

You have begun your journey of transforming your consciousness with the Will to Harmonise. It is the quality of Divine Will that guides the soul of humanity right now – harmony through conflict and the creation of beauty through merging the inner life with the outer life. What follows are ways to call upon this great force to bring more beauty, harmony, balance, and unity into your life.

■

6

Confirm Wishes to Reality

Our wishes, or desires, are one of the defining attributes of our individuality, but how many people can make their dreams come true? In truth, many people don't even know what they really want, much less how to accomplish their goals. There are others who know exactly what they want, but still can't quite get their act together to accomplish their heart's desire. The idea of wish fulfilment is something which first enters human consciousness at an early age indeed.

In fact, we all learn to desire long before we learn to speak. We form wordless impressions of what we want, or don't want, and this is the earliest concept we have of the subject. These impressions persist, and they constitute part of the underlying structure which shapes all our future wishes.

From the moment we are born, most of us begin to

wish for the warm, safe environment of the womb, from which we have been violently pushed, or pulled, into this world. The personality we form, from that moment on, is largely shaped by our desires. These fall into two broad categories, those things we'd like to have more of, and those things we'd rather be rid of, or get away from. In general, people feel that they are attracted to pleasurable things, and try to avoid painful things, but it doesn't always work as we expect it to. As long as we continue to be attracted or repelled, however, we will continue to endeavor to satisfy the desires which arise as a result.

We develop theories in our mind, about what actions might yield worthwhile results, as infants, long before we have any concept of what words mean, but we soon learn to use words in our strategy to gain our heart's desire.

At some point, words and actions become connected, as we find that there is a word for almost anything we can do, or possess. Later, as we learn more complex behaviours, we are supplied with phrases and sentences to describe them, and other things, as well.

But this also gives each of us tools to aid in obtaining what we wish to have in our life. On the other hand, where words bring us some things, they don't help us to obtain other things at all. Many things are possible to attain, or obtain, only if we take correct action, at the right time and place.

Sometimes strategies that work well with one person,

or one group of people, are poorly adapted to the temperament of another, and it makes life tough to understand. Similarly, differing situations demand different solutions to the same problem. It seems there is no universal formula for success, but rather a range of approaches particularly well suited to a variety of temperaments and environments.

Although there is no single strategy for getting what you want, which works for all people and all situations, certain elements of strategy are useful to remember, and will help you to find the best approach to a given task. The idea is not merely to adopt a policy, however, based on someone else's method, but to find out what works for you, and make that your method.

Some steps

The first step is knowing what you really want, and this often isn't so obvious as it seems, because most of us are too caught up in the activity of living life to step back from our immediate conditions and ask ourselves such a basic question. If you knew that anything was possible, and you could have exactly what you most desire, what would you wish for? If you had no limits whatsoever, what would you do? If there are things you have always wanted, places you've always wanted to go, or people you would really like to see, its better to know that, than to turn away from your heart's desires because they appear unattainable, but take care that you wish for things you would still want if you actually had them. Sometimes what you wish for, at one point, will continue coming to you long after your desire for that special thing, or for the individual you longed to meet, has faded.

This doesn't mean that wishing alone, or having a clear concept of what you are wishing for, is going to bring your wish to life.

Of course, everyone can wish for things which they have no immediate way of obtaining, and you can never have as much as you can wish for, but almost anything worth doing can be accomplished, and virtually anything worth having can be obtained by combining imagination and persistent effort, over a period of time, with some amount of cooperation.

Be sure, however, that you are wishing for things that don't require other people to behave exactly as you would like. It's better to wish for what allows you to do your own thing, and allows others to respond as they feel is appropriate. By so doing, you leave room for their individuality in your plans, and you don't leave yourself open for blame. In my opinion, this is the only way to go.

The second step is focusing your desires, or clarifying your intent. You need to sift through the vast expanse of feelings within you, as well as looking to the outside world, to find the things which are most urgent, what has lasting importance, what can be done right now to help your situation, and so on. Where the assessment of what you want should be more of a free-for-all, with the idea of discovering your fondest wishes and dreams, the second step is more of a sobering look at how some of your most cherished desires can be worked into the scheme of your real-life activity.

While going through this part of the process, you must be both thoroughly realistic and affirmative. It is extremely important to make sure that, when you are done, all of your goals are phrased clearly, and positively, so that your sub-conscious will get the right message. The sub-conscious mind responds quite literally, so we must be careful about how we describe what we desire.

We wish to avoid telling ourselves what not to do, or what we think we sort of want, and learn to give our nervous systems a clear picture of exactly what it is that we do want. In order to accomplish this, we need to use accurately descriptive language, rather than suggestive but nebulous phrasing, and we need to describe what we want to have, want to do, and want to be, not those things we wish to leave behind. Rather than saying "I want to stop smoking," for example, one can dwell on those things you will do instead of smoking. Perhaps "I will do deep breathing whenever I get the urge to smoke." would be a suitable affirmation for someone attempting to stop. Memory studies have shown that forgetful people actually tend to remind themselves to leave things behind (i.e., "I just know I'll forget my umbrella."), and so on. This doesn't help much at all. Clear, and positive, instructions will put your sub-conscious to work for you, instead. All of your goals should be phrased in this manner, if you wish for them to become realities.

When you have completely evaluated and organised your wishes, you should be able to write down four or five things you can do right now (or in the near future) which will both improve your immediate situation, and bring you closer to achieving some of your fondest wishes in your lifetime.

What is most important is that you know what you wish to do, but writing it down can empower the mind's focusing ability to work for you. People with written goals tend to do measurably better with them than people who don't write goals down, and there are good reasons why, but the choice is yours. Make sure that you are fairly thorough, in any case, going through each step of the process. Creating the outcomes you desire requires that you be both specific, and realistic.

Having vague, conflicted, or impossible notions is not the way to succeed. You want to make sure that you're not being superficial, either in assessing your own true feelings, or in dealing with real-world complexities. After all, your own satisfaction is what's at stake.

The third step involves using both effort and imagination to bring your plans to fruition. Specifically, you must work both toward your goals and from your goals, to ensure success in your endeavours. It is also helpful to harness the power of both incentive and fear, as motivators, to get you where you want to be. Most people are well versed in the first approach, the slow building of momentum by taking care of one detail after another, until all of the necessary conditions for creating the final product have been met. Fewer people have mastered the second technique, which involves picturing yourself in the world where your goals have already been achieved, and then looking backwards, toward the present, to see what steps were taken to get there. It's important, in this case, to feel good about what you desire.

Any approach which doesn't figure fear into the equation, however, has the potential for problems. Fear can be a killer, it is true, but it doesn't have to be. Sometimes fear can be a good thing, as it is justifiably one of the most powerful motivators of all. The trick is to use its power to your advantage, to inspire courage, rather than allowing it to intimidate you, or prompt you to be foolhardy. Using both incentive and fear allows both possibility and necessity to move you forward.

Each approach has to be used interactively to be useful at all. By this, we mean that when the first results are not what we expect, we must alter our approach somewhat. Every step taken will provide feedback of our efforts, and supply us with additional information which can help us to adjust and improve our strategies for success. In addition, combining the different approaches in creative ways will allow you to create a kind of synergy between your inward and outward processes, where what is learned from one approach is swiftly applied to aid the other, saving you from wasting precious effort or scarce resources. Clear imagination of your goals can save you steps in the 'real' world, at times, but swift, effective, action can free up your creativity for more interesting, or more important, problems.

Likewise, a clear incentive to act, in terms of the enjoyment gained by possible rewards, is always helpful, but the feeling of necessity to act, resulting from fear of possible consequences, is often essential to the process of making progress. We use what works for us, but every angle to play is one more tool to aid in the process of realising our goals, and each has its place, for dealing with the various challenges we encounter, on the road to creating the life we want.

Any approach requires some level of participation or involvement, and therefore one needs to be motivated, or at least willing to apply oneself. The question of how invigorated one needs to be for optimum performance is somewhat tricky, however. You see, not only do certain tasks or situations require a particularly relaxed, or vigorous, approach to a problem, but different people also require different levels of motivation to achieve the same result.

Where some need to psych themselves up, and generate enthusiasm to do their best work, this is a total waste of time for others. Sometimes being too keyed-up can make a task more difficult, or even impossible. Too much effort can burn one out prematurely, and too strong a motivation can create fear or tension. Not enough effort, or motivation, may result in no progress at all. There is, however, an optimum state of arousal for a specific person to complete a given task. The trick to achieving any desired result is knowing what that proper level of activation is, and being just that excited, whether the effort required is mental or physical. How highly charged do we really need to be to excel? Exactly enough to get ourselves to take effective action. Working well, therefore, means the intelligent use of effort.

Working toward a goal involves creating, acquiring, or assembling the necessary pieces of the puzzle you are trying to solve. By building up the necessary resources, whether they are materials and tools, or blueprints and schematics, we actually create opportunities which did not exist before.

By fulfiling prerequisite conditions for our endeavours, we provide a solid foundation to build upon, giving us something to work from in order to make our wishes a reality. We also obtain a visible and tangible representation of our progress, as we accumulate material, or situational, evidence for our efforts. Every little success along the way tends to add to both our momentum, and our motivation.

Of course, acquiring the necessary skills to work with the resources you possess is also a process of building toward the desired state. By practicing the necessary skills and actions until we are certain that we can handle whatever is required, we can strengthen our foundation, creating an even greater opportunity to make our wishes a reality. Best of all, this kind of result (experience) becomes a part of us, so that it can be applied to future goals, or future attempts at the same goals.

Working from the goal involves attracting the pieces of the puzzle to you, rather than attempting to pursue them. The image of your goal becomes like a homing beacon, inviting you to step forward on the path to success. A clear picture of the outcome you wish to create will do far more than increase your desire to get there, however.

Imagining the wish fulfilled will empower you by allowing you to enhance the probability that the desired outcome will take place, and it also allows you to answer two very important questions. The first is "How do I know when I get there?", and the other is "What do I do when I get there?."

By taking the time to imagine the situation you want to create, you have the opportunity to address both of these issues, as many times as you like, before being faced with the situation of either falling short of, or overshooting, your goal, or missing a golden opportunity because you didn't know how to deal with the situation when you arrive.

Too many people don't have a clear concept of how to recognise success, once they have reached it, and many more don't know what to do next, once their plans are exhausted. It is wise to have a clear concept of both, although you don't need to work out all the details.

Using the imagination is much more powerful than depending upon will power alone. By utilising will power for working toward a goal, you can make yourself strive for what you want, but working from a goal can make the goal work for you, by serving to motivate and lend meaning to your participation, as long as you continue to envision it! The general rule is that the more vividly you can imagine the outcome you desire, the more likely you are to see it manifest in real life.

If you can put yourself in your future shoes easily, and can experience all of the sounds, sights, and even the smell of being there, you are probably well within reach of your goals. If, on the other hand, you have a hard time picturing anything but how your plans could fall apart, don't be disheartened. That which you fear is seldom the only possibility. It is usually only part of a range of possible outcomes.

When you continue to exercise your imagination, or just entertain the appropriate (and effectively phrased) questions a little bit longer (to see other possible outcomes), you will find that all of the positive possibilities will appear in your imagination, in their turn.

Sometimes the fear of failure is a gift, in that it can be your mind's way of attempting to guide you past the obstacles to success, or keep you from inflicting harm upon yourself. In other cases, it reflects inhibitory conditioning, that was inflicted upon us in childhood through guilt or intimidation, which was used to keep us in line, and make us more easily controlled, by parents, teachers, and other authority figures.

In still other cases, the fear arises out of an unconscious attempt to sabotage our own success, because we don't believe in what we are trying to do, or don't actually desire the outcome we are ostensibly striving for. In some instances, it is a representation of our darker side, as we don't believe in ourselves, or don't consider ourselves worthy of the accomplishment for which we are making an effort.

In most cases, however, the fear we feel can be used as a motivating factor, because it arises as a result of the fact that we want something better than what we fear, and our mind is trying to show us what will happen, if we fail to take action, or fail to imagine something better. In virtually every situation where fear arises, moreover, it is trying to give us a message.

Usually, the best way to deal with fear is to come to terms with it, rather than to confront or avoid it. Sometimes it is wise to "imagine the worst," and become OK with that, so that we can defuse the emotional charge which would otherwise keep us stuck in unproductive, or even life threatening, circumstances, but it is usually best not to settle for that alone, when better options exist. This is where having the courage to take action becomes crucially important. Allowing fear to intimidate and immobilize you, so that you are prevented from taking action, will certainly not aid your cause, or carry you forward to success. Merely being at peace with your fears does little for you, in attempts to fulfill your desires. Nor does it make sense to go forth in blind anger, lashing out at everything, and everyone, that appears to be in your way.

This may produce results, but they are seldom totally positive. A consistent effort to do what you can do, coupled with efforts to discover, and/or imagine, alternatives which may yield results, and the creation of plans which lead to superior outcomes, is the appropriate middle path between defective and excessive action.

Of course, there are times when no amount of individual effort or imagination is going to be enough, and the fulfilment of your wish will require more resources than you possess.

What are you supposed to do then? The answer is usually that you need to get the help, and cooperation, of other people. This raises the questions of how to ask for things, what to ask for, whom to ask, and so on. There is also a question of cost. You need to discover what the people you are asking require of you, and learn how to fulfill those needs, if you wish for them to give you what you want, in return.

Don't mis-apply the Golden Rule, by offering others

what you think they'd want if they were you. If you expect to get what you need from others, give those people what they really want, by finding out first what that is, and then seeking ways to help them get it. Without this, we have no right to expect the cooperation of those whose help we seek.

When asking for the help of others, you need to be willing to give something in return. Sometimes, you must be prepared to create value for the other person ahead of time, for them to be willing to help you. Knowing what you want from them, and what they want from you, is the first step in creating an agreement which will fulfil your wishes.

Then, of course, you must know how to ask for what you desire, or what will bring you closer to that. You may wish to consider, however, if the person you are asking is capable of granting your wish, at all, in the first place. Sometimes, a lot of time can be wasted trying to secure an agreement from parties who can't really deliver what is required. It is almost always best to ask someone who can actually give you what you want. Failing to take this into consideration is one of the most common reasons people don't realise their goals.

How to ask for what you wish is an art in itself, and there are many ways to approach it, depending on who you are, what you are asking for, and who you are asking. In every case, the process of asking requires thought, or planning, and timing as well. You should tailor your request, and its presentation, to the actual conditions and participants. Get to know them. It's good to have a specific way (possibly even two, or three, ways) of asking for what you desire worked out ahead of time. It also helps to apply the imaginative technique here, by asking yourself the question of how the other individual(s) might respond, and envisioning how you would deal with different responses.

Then, you may wish to practice speaking your request a few times, to see if it actually sounds as good when you say it as it does in your mind, or on paper. Presenting your idea as effectively as possible may require both the spoken word, and words on paper, or diagrams, and so on.

Even the most excellent presentation of the best product, or the best ideas, however, will fall on deaf ears sometimes. Unfortunately, this happens quite often. In some cases, the other party isn't looking for what you have to offer, or just isn't prepared to invest in your plans at this time. This only means you need to try again later, ask someone else, or perhaps change your requirements. Be as persistent as you need to be, but without making a nuisance of yourself.

Do more on your own. Keep trying variations on your basic theme, until you find something that works for you. Remember that some of the world's greatest success stories began with rather humble, or even daunting, conditions. Those who persisted, despite the difficulties they had, almost always achieved something worthwhile. People have the power to accomplish almost anything, if they keep trying long enough. There are some situations, however, where there are no more options to try. What do we do, in that case?

How about getting help from a higher source? Is it meaningful for an individual to seek inspiration from beyond, or from deep within? Does the Universe respond to our beliefs and desires? Can we tap into a greater inner power by tuning-in to the forming power of the universe, nature, and life itself? The answer to all of these questions is yes, to some degree, but each person's ability to create an advantage by doing so is dependent on a number of factors. To receive inspiration, for instance, you must have a quiet enough mind to allow new thoughts to surface. To get the universe to respond to your wishes, you must ask for its assistance. To take advantage of the forces of nature, you must be in harmony with the natural order. Knowing the natural laws helps some things greatly. This includes knowing the laws of the mind (individual and universal), as well as science. If you are looking for divine intervention, having a personal relationship with the Divinity can help quite a bit. In a similar way as with people, knowing how to ask for divine help is a useful art too.

The idea of using prayers, wishes, or spells to bring things into your life which you wouldn't have otherwise is not a new one. Nor is this approach totally without merit. In fact, it seems that the universe does respond to our wishes, in some measure, whether we like it or not, and regardless of if we notice. Some people believe that the universal mind acts upon all our thoughts, feelings, and desires automatically.

Others would say that God listens to all our prayers, and knows our heart's desire. In either case, our beliefs are seen as the key factor in determining what we receive from life. How would we know this, if it were true? Could such a state be concealed? If you were all powerful, but considered your attempts to exercise power to be futile, and all your efforts to succeed destined for failure, what results would you achieve? You might very well create a world of difficulties for yourself, where your belief in your own powerlessness, and in your likelihood of failure, would make that real for you. If, instead, your belief is that God provides all you could want, that the Goddess is sharing her abundance, or merely that Life is bountiful, this may create something very different.

The question arises of whether prayers, wishes, and spells, are an ethical way to pursue ones goals. Do we have a right to impose our own desires upon the lives of others, assuming we have the ability to do so? Is it appropriate to bend the rules, if we can, so that the natural order serves our wishes? Mormons believe that it is our duty to ask God for that which we want in our life, in order to provide for our families, and assist the rest of mankind.

Followers of Islam, on the other hand, state both their

prayers, and their promises to others, in terms that let God decide (i.e., - I will see you next month, if it is the will of Allah (God)). I personally believe that either approach can be both effective and that prayer is appropriate, if done in a spirit of reverence, and caring for all of life.

Some people take this attitude of reverence to another level, asking for nothing specifically that is for themselves, but proclaiming "I want only what is for the highest and best." Pagans, on the other hand, proclaim "As you harm noone, do what you will." I believe that divine help is always available, and that it's our right to have that help. We are powerful beings, with a natural magic of our own, but others stand ready. Angels will come to assist you, if you need them, but usually come only if invited.

Whether we call the approach of working with a higher power magic, prayer, or merely wishful thinking, the process is largely the same. Some skeptics will claim that there is no reasonable basis for this belief, but this is not the case.

Where there may be no definitive scientific proof, and there are certainly many charlatans out there, there is both evidence and a theoretical basis for the existence of psychic powers, miracles, magic, and spiritual phenomena. Science has made discoveries indicating that consciousness itself creates results. In fact, the role of the observer as determiner has come to the fore as one of the most fundamental principles of Quantum

Mechanics. It seems that one can't observe most sub-atomic processes without influencing the outcome, and some processes are so sensitive that even the possibility of observing the outcome is enough to change the nature of what is observed completely. This appears to show that our universe is strongly influenced by the perceptual strategies of conscious beings. What we do to merely observe something can markedly change the manifested result. Imagine what our conscious efforts might do, if they were properly focused.

Of course, events and processes at our scale are rather different from sub-atomic events, but all of our universe is created and sustained through energy exchanges which manifest as sub-atomic, atomic, or molecular, quantum-mechanical processes. It appears likely that thoughts, and even consciousness itself, may be quantum-mechanical in nature. In this case, it makes perfect sense that changing the quantum-mechanical vibrations of our thinking would effect changes in the world around us, as well.

Thus, there may be a scientific basis for many kinds of psychic phenomena, spiritual experiences, miracles, and magic. I do not mean to say that all such events are genuine, but rather that the findings of Modern Science appear to require the possibility for such things to occur. If these methods work at all, they can be of great value when no other options exist. It is my personal belief that the benefits can be greater still, when one keeps this channel open by regular use.

Whether the approach to problems is esoteric or purely pragmatic, however, it is often not a matter of what we wish for, do, or provide, at all, which determines our success. Sometimes what we have to eliminate is equally important to what we need to add. In fact, it is often far more important. Removing roadblocks to success makes it unnecessary to get around problematic situations, or to build bridges over them.

In this way, the proper solution can be simplicity itself. Often enough, all we need to do is get out of our own way, or clear away the opposing elements, in order to have what we want from life. This can be called following the path of least resistance, since what we need to do, in order to accomplish things this way, is merely to reduce the level of internal and external resistance, until things happen naturally. By simply relaxing, and going with the flow, we can have things which would otherwise remain forever out of our grasp, and that is the beauty of this path.

We can all have more of what we wish for in our lives, and that is why we have desires in the first place. Don't be ashamed to want things, and don't be afraid to receive them, or to have them. If you are willing to encourage yourself to dream your dreams, and then to take what action is appropriate, you can see your wishes fulfilled, but first you must let it be OK to want.

Give yourself permission to have desires, as this too is part of the process of fulfilment. Desire arises naturally, and it is nothing to be ashamed of. Wish fulfilment is possible only for those who can accept this. Even the most highly evolved people still have desire, in some form. We may choose to pursue noble goals exclusively, but in order to achieve them, we still have to want something. Only by honoring our desires can we hope to see our wishes fulfilled. This is, perhaps, the most important key of all. By taking our own desires seriously, and using them to help shape our plans effectively, we can accomplish all that is possible. When we give our desires wings, by using our thoughts, feelings, and actions together, in harmony, the sky is the limit of our potential.

■

7

Everything Happens for the Good Reason

In our opinion and even from our personal experiences, even negative experiences often have some kind of important wisdom that you should take from it to help you in whatever it is that you are trying to accomplish.

In that sense, a bad experience is really something good in disguise and it's up to you to reveal that. A very typical example that we hear a lot in business is that a person starting out gets completely frustrated as it seems like every vendor/supplier he works with ends up not providing him with what he wanted and so there is no point in trying anymore.

That is the easy thing to do by simply looking at the event from a negative perspective as if it didn't help you at all. It also creates a false belief that it's always the other person's fault.

But really, even with that example you can find something good out of it. For example, that could be a lesson for you to thoroughly write down what you are looking for in the future and to create a contract agreement to prevent any surprises on what was said before. If you think about it, it's a great thing that you learned to do that now as oppose later when you have to do something bigger which could potentially cause you to lose a lot more.

Can it really be true that everything happens for a reason? As amazing as it sounds, it is. There is significance in every event of our lives, from the most joyful and empowering to the inexplicable or seemingly unjust.

Is it really true that everything happens for a reason? After all, that's an amazing thing to say-that no matter what happens to you, not only does something valuable come out of it but it's just what you need.

Of course, sometimes it's easy for us to believe that everything happens for a reason. We see it in little ways, like when our plans for an evening out fall through at the last minute, and we discover that everything we really want is at home that night anyway.

And sometimes we see it in not-so-little ways. A woman wrenched her back and had to spend a month in bed. She felt this was the last thing she needed in her life, particularly since it happened at a time when she had to make some important decisions. And then it hit her-this was exactly what she needed. Her old habit had been to rush impetuously into a new decision without thinking it through. Now it was as if life were saying, "If you won't give yourself time to think, I will."

We very much want to believe that the things that happen to us have great meaning. It's the way we feel life should be. Yes, some days we feel our life's a soap opera. But we want-we need-to have the sense that there's a purpose and value to it all. And we're right.

Be assured that:

When you discover the true meaning of the events in your life, everything changes.

You feel stronger because your sense that everything has meaning gives you great confidence.

You feel wiser because you see how everything connects.

You're more in touch with who you are because you know that you're living the life you were meant to lead.

And you're happier because you're able to put your loss behind you and have a sense of a future filled with good things.

Until you get to this place, nothing is going to feel

right. Let's say you're outdoors and you suddenly feel a drop of moisture fall on your head. You're not going to be able to think of anything else until you figure out why that happened.

Is water dripping from some air conditioner up high? Is it starting to rain? Is a flying monkey peeing on your head? You have to know why that drop of moisture fell on your head because you can't feel safe going forward until you do.

We need to know why much more when what fell on our heads is a catastrophe. If you can't make sense of the catastrophe, it's as if your life is mere dice on a crap table– if nothing has any meaning, everything's random, anything can happen.

It's painful to live not knowing why you got so sick that time or why you lost the love of your life–much more painful than people suspect. One woman was flying home for Thanksgiving when she was in college.

As the plane was flying along twenty thousand feet in the air, she developed a terrible earache. But that's not what made her cry. In the dark of a night-time flight she was sobbing because there was pain like this in the world, seemingly without any rhyme or reason.

One guy described this feeling differently: "When I think about the bad stuff that's happened in my life, I feel I'm just a goddamn fool of the cosmos. It's humiliating! On a sidewalk crowded with people, I'm the one who's stepped in the dog poop. No one else is as stupid or unlucky as I am. The problem is: How can I go forward, how can I trust the future if I feel I am this stupid unlucky guy?"

Knowing that there's a reason for what happens also saves us from being filled with blame. Blame is a very human attempt to make sense of some catastrophe, but most of the time we hate the way it feels.

And yet when something bad happens to us, it's almost a reflex to think, It's because everyone hates me, because I'm a loser, because I'm doomed. And so the blame begins.

We blame other people, and then we end up with the sense that the world is full of bad people. We blame ourselves, and then instead of feeling healthy, strong, and whole we see ourselves as sick, weak, and broken. And we blame life itself. What could be more demoralising than feeling condemned to having bad things always happen to us and not being able to do anything about it?

Blame is like a boomerang that loops around and bonks us on the noggin. Try this yourself: If you see someone struggling with sadness, anxiety, and negativity, listen to his story. You'll soon see he's living in a world where all he sees are things to blame because he lives without positive meanings for what's happened to him. The only cure is to restore the sense that there is a good reason for everything that happens.

Lots of things happen to us that challenge our sense that everything happens for a reason. It can be anything. You get seriously ill at the worst possible moment. You think you've found the love of your life but something goes haywire between you and now the two of you are over. You've had one of those really painful childhoods. You screw up and lose a lot of money. Someone you love dies.

Yeah, we think, maybe there's a meaning for some things that happen, but not for this. And even if we still have a shred of faith left that there is meaning in these events, we don't know how to find it.

After all, the events in our lives don't come to us with labels attached telling us what they mean. We can spend years searching in vain. We ask friends, but they haven't gone through what we have. We ask someone who has gone through something similar, but that person is probably struggling to find meaning, too.

Sometimes people come into your life and you know right away that they were meant to be there to serve some sort of purpose, teach you a lesson or help figure out who you are or who you want to become. You never know who these people may be but when you look eyes with them, you know that every moment that you are with them, they will affect your life in some profound way. And sometimes things happen to you at the time that may seem horrible, painful and unfair, but in reflection you realise that without overcoming those obstacles you would have never realised your potential, strength, will power or heart.

Everything happens for a reason! Nothing happens by chance or by means of good luck. Illness, injury, love, lost moments of true greatness and sheer stupidity all occur to test the limits of your soul. Without these small tests, life would be like a smoothly paved, straight, flat road to nowhere, safe and comfortable but dull and utterly pointless. The people you meet affect your life. The successes and downfalls that you experience can create who you are, and the bad experiences can be learned from.... In fact, they are probably the most poignant and important ones. If someone hurts you, betrays you or breaks your heart, forgive them because they have helped you learn about trust and the importance of being cautious to whom you open your heart. If someone loves you, love them back unconditionally not only because they love you, but also because they are teaching you to love and open your heart and eyes to little things.

Make everyday count. Appreciate every moment and take from it everything that you possibly can, for you may never be able to experience it again. Talk to people who you have never talked to before, and actually listen.

Let yourself fall in love, even if it doesn't seem right

because you are too young or too far, just follow your heart. Surround yourself with those who make you smile, laugh, and make you happy.

Break free and set your sights high. Hold your head up because you have every right to. Tell yourself you are a great individual and believe in yourself, for if you don't believe in yourself, no one else will believe in you. Create your own life then let go and live it.

8

Modern Thoughts on Good Living

There are nine basic perceptions about good living. Just have a look on these nine thoughts.

1. Creator, or the Ultimate Source, or the All That Is All, or the Universal Creative Impulse, or God, or whatever you may wish to name it, desires your prosperity and success. It does not desire (or demand) any impoverishment, suffering or limitation of any kind for you UNLESS that is what you desire or envision for yourself. Creator wants you to be blessed, wants you to succeed, wants you to have all the wealth and abundance you desire for yourself. Desire is de-sire... of the father. Your desires for wealth and abundance are divine. Honour them.

2. You are an inseparable part of Source. You are a divine creator as well as a sacred creature. Your intimate connection with the All That Is All is always there

and cannot ever be severed for any reason EXCEPT that you will it to be so. (and even that is an illusion) You don't need to do anything to return to Source. You are already there and always have been and always will be at one with The All That Is All. You are a part of, not apart from, Infinite Intelligence. Your consciousness is contained within universal consciousness. Each and every thought held in your consciousness is an integral part of the universal. It adds to the whole. It is creative.

3.   You deserve success and wealth. You do not need to measure up to any standard, not even the ones you have set for yourself in order to merit wealth, success or happiness. Abundance is your birthright as a child of God. There is no prime cause at work that denies you the fulfilment of your fondest desires for success and happiness. To the contrary, the universe is set up to support your abundance. Harmonise yourself with the way the universe works and you will have all you envision and desire. It's all about vibration and harmonics.

4.   The Law of Attraction is always working. Whatever you have in your life right now, you have attracted into it. You do not attract what you wish for or even what you envision; you attract what you are. What you have and what you see around you is but a reflection of who you are being in this moment. Denial does not negate the Law of Attraction anymore than it negates Gravity, which is, after all,

just another example of the Law of Attraction in action. Become more and you will have more.

5.   The choice is always yours. At each and every moment, you have the power to choose to be, do and have more. Or less. Whatever you can imagine, you can have. The four principle forces that power your creativity are: thought, belief, desire and intent. You can choose what and how to think. You can choose what and how to believe. You can choose what to desire. You can choose your intentions. Such is your power. Choose carefully. Choose intentionally. Choose purposefully. Your choices of thought, belief, desire and intent determine who you are. Who you are determines what you get to have.

6.   The true purpose of your life is simply to revere, relish and contribute. Life is meant to be a joyful event. When you honor all things, especially yourself, as being sacred; and when you wholeheartedly partake in and appreciate the pleasures of life; and when you consciously and intentionally choose to make a contribution to life you are fulfilling the purpose of your life and you will experience joy and fulfilment.

When you are searching for the purpose of your life, you are seeking the way that you can make a contribution or express your gratitude for the gift of life. Become a blessing and you will be blessed.

7.   Love really is all you need. Compassion will open you up to being able to receive and accept all the

love, joy and abundance that surrounds you constantly. Compassion for all creation, most especially for your sacred self, is the key that unlocks the door into infinity. Infinite love surrounds you. Be compassionate to life. Become passionate about life and you will experience all the abundance you are willing to allow yourself. In order to love your neighbour as yourself, you need to first love yourself. Love you. Honour you. Cherish you.

8.   When you remember these simple things, life makes sense; when you forget them, you get confused by the apparent complexity. You wrote this script, now you are acting it out as the ultimate method actor.

However, you may stumble occasionally, in the brilliance of your performance, when you forget the plot. Since you wrote this script, you can change it at any time you desire. Since you are playing the role you wrote, you can play it any way you think best. Drama, comedy, tragedy, romance, adventure, soap opera? You decide.

9.   You are hearing this now because you asked to be reminded, from time to time, of what you know, but sometimes forget, as you immerse yourself in the experience of life on planet earth. You came here to play this game. That was your original choice. It remains your choice.

Some important instructions for good life

Give people more than they expect and do it cheerfully.

Don't believe all you hear, spend all you have or sleep all you want.

When you say, "I love you", mean it.

When you say, "I'm sorry", look the person in the eye.

Never laugh at anyone's dreams.

In disagreements, fight fairly. No name calling.

Talk slow but think quick.

When someone asks you a question you don't want to answer, smile and ask, "Why do you want to know?"

Remember that great love and great achievements involve great risk.

When you lose, don't lose the lesson.

Remember the three R's: Respect for self; Respect for others; Responsibility for all your actions.

When you realise you've made a mistake, take immediate steps to correct it.

Spend some time alone.

Open your arms to change, but don't let go of your values.

Remember that silence is sometimes the best answer.

Live a good, honourable life. Then when you get older and think back, you'll get to enjoy it a second time.

A loving atmosphere in your home is so important. Do all you can to create a tranquil harmonious home.

In disagreements with loved ones, deal with the current situation. Don't bring up the past.

Read between the lines.

Share your knowledge. It's a way to achieve immortality.

Be gentle with the earth.

Pray. There's immeasurable power in it.

Never interrupt when you are being flattered.

Mind your own business.

If you make a lot of money, put it to use helping others while you are living. That is wealth's greatest satisfaction.

Judge your success by what you had to give up in order to get it.

Remember that your character is your destiny.

Modern thoughts on Living

We create our own reality by the thoughts, beliefs, intentions and expectations that we hold. This hypothesis has been part of Eastern thought and religion for centuries, and has recently established a growing following in the West. Its essence can be seen in the works of many respected thinkers of our time, including members of the scientific community. And it was a major influence in the birth of Spirit to Spirit. Some important thoughts based on modern thinking are as follows:

"In each life you choose and create your own settings or environments; and in this one you chose your parents and whatever cnildhood incidents that came within your experience.

You wrote the script. Like a true absent minded professor, the conscious self forgets all this, however, so when tragedy appears in the script, difficulty or challenges, the conscious self looks for someone or something to blame."

"Using your free will, you have made physical reality into something quite different than what was intended. You have allowed the ego to become overly developed and specialised.

You were here to work out problems and challenges, but you were always to be aware of your own inner reality, and of your nonphysical existence. To a large extent you have lost contact with this. You have focused so strongly upon physical reality that it become the only reality that you know."

"If you do not like the state of your world, it is you yourselves that must change, individually and en masse. This is the only way that change will be effected."

"The responsibility for your life and your world is

indeed yours. You form your own dreams and you form your own physical reality. The world is the physical materialisation of the inner selves which you have formed."

"Your must honour yourselves and see within yourselves the spirit of eternal validity. You must honour all other individuals, because within each is the spark of this validity."

"Do not fall into the old ways that will lead you precisely into the world that you fear. There is no man who hates but that hatred is reflected outward and made physical, and there is no man who loves but that love is reflected outward and made physical."

"Beyond myself there is another self and still another, of which I am aware. And that self tells you that there is a reality beyond human reality and experience that cannot be made verbal or translated into human terms."

"Seth is what I am, yet I am more than Seth is. ... Names are arbitrary, and we use them merely for your convenience. Seth's name or mine isn't important."

"Identity and consciousness existed long before your earth was formed. Consciousness is the force behind matter, and it forms many other realities besides the physical one. So much of your energy is used in the physical productions that you cannot afford to perceive any reality but your own."

"The human race is a stage through which various

forms of consciousness travel. Yours is a training system for emerging consciousness, you must first learn to handle energy and see through physical materialisation, the concrete result of thought and emotion."

"In the most basic sense, the purpose of life is being – as opposed to not being. In your system of three – dimensional reality you are learning about mental energy (also called thought energy or psychic energy) and how to use it."

"Knowledge about mental energy and its use is learned by constantly transforming your thoughts and emotions into physical form (your physical reality) and by then perceiving and dealing with the matter and events that are formed."

"From doing this, you are supposed to get a clear picture of your inner development as it is reflected by the exterior environment. You participate in physical reality so that you can operate and experience within this dimension. Here, you can develop your abilities, learn, create, solve problems and help others."

"Matter is the shape that basic experience takes when it comes into your three-dimensional system. Your dreams, thoughts, expectations, beliefs and emotions are literally transformed into physical matter."

"Every nerve and fibre within the body has an unseen inner purpose. Nerve impulses travel outward from the body, along invisible pathways, in much the same manner that they travel within the body."

"These pathways are carriers of telepathic thoughts, impulses, and desires containing all the codified data necessary for translating any thought or image into physical actuality, altering seemingly objective events."

"This telepathy operates constantly at an "automatic" or subconscious level, providing communication to back up sensory data. Telepathy is the glue that holds the physical universe in position, so that you can agree on the existence and properties of objects."

"The physical environment is as much a part of you as your own body. What seems to be a perception, an objective concrete event independent from you, is instead the materialisation of your own emotions, energy and mental environment."

"Events and objects are actually focal points where highly charged psychic impulses are transformed into something that can be physically perceived: a breakthrough into matter."

"The intensity of a thought or image largely determines the immediacy of the physical materialisation. All such images or thoughts are not completely materialised, in your perception, as their intensity may be too weak."

"If you want to know what you think of yourself, then

ask yourself what you think of others and you will find the answer."

"True self-knowledge is indispensable for health and vitality. The recognition of the truth about the self simply means that you must first find out what you think about yourself subconsciously. If it is a good image, build upon it. If it is a poor one, recognise it as only the opinion you have held of yourself and not an absolute state."

"You are not your emotions. They flow through you, you feel them and then they disappear. When you try to hold them back they build up."

"You must learn to trust your own spontaneous nature. Your nervous system knows how to react. It reacts spontaneously when you allow it to. In spontaneity there is a discipline that utterly escapes you, and an order beyond any that you know. Spontaneity knows its own order."

"All of nature is spontaneous. Our bodies will be healthy automatically if we do not project false ideas upon them. Physical symptoms are communications from the inner self, indications that we are making mental errors of one kind or another.

Do not forget that you are a part of the inner self. Search yourself for the inner problem represented by the symptoms, and measure your progress as the symptoms subside."

"You sell yourself short if you believe that you are only a physical organism living within the boundaries cast upon you by time and space."

"You are a unique individual. You form your physical environment. You are part of all that is. There is no place within you that creativity does not exist."

Thoughts on Beliefs and Expectations

"You create your reality according to your beliefs and expectations; therefore you should examine these carefully. If you do not like some aspect of your world, then examine your own expectations."

"Realise that your physical experience and environment is the materialisation of your beliefs. If you find great exuberance, health, effective work, abundance, smiles on the faces of those who you meet, then take it for granted that your beliefs are beneficial. If you see a world that is good, people like you, take it for granted again, that your beliefs are beneficial.

But if you find poor health, a lack of meaningful work, a lack of abundance, a world of sorrow and evil, then assume your beliefs are faulty and begin examining them."

"Your world is formed in faithful replica of your own thoughts. If you think positive suggestions to yourself about a situation you send telepathic ammunition for positive use. You must learn to erase a negative thought or picture by replacing it with its opposite."

"You should tell yourself frequently 'I will only react to constructive suggestions.' This gives you positive ammunition against your own negative thoughts and those of others."

"A negative thought, if not erased, will almost certainly result in a negative condition. Say to yourself, 'That is in the past. Now in this new moment, this new present, I am already beginning to hangs for the better.'"

"It does not do to repress negative thoughts, such as fears, angers, or resentment. They should be recognised, faced and replaced. Recognise resentment when it is felt, and then realise that resentment can be dismissed. Initial recognition must be made. Then you must imagine removing the resentment 'by its roots' and replacing it with a positive feeling."

"You must watch the pictures that you paint with your imagination. Your environment and the conditions of your life at any given time are the direct result of your own inner expectations. If you imagine dire circumstances, ill health or desperate loneliness, these will be automatically materialised, for these thoughts themselves bring about the conditions that will give them a reality in physical terms. If you would have good health then you must imagine this as vividly as you fearfully imagine ill health."

"You create your own difficulties. This is true for each individual. The inner psychological state is projected outward, gaining physical reality – whatever the psychological state may be. You cannot escape your own attitudes, for they will form the nature of what you see. If changes are to occur, they must be mental and psychic changes. These will be reflected in your environment. Negative, distrustful, fearful, or degrading attitudes toward anyone work against the self."

Thoughts on the Inner Self

"The ego at any give time in this life is simply the part of the inner self that surfaces in physical reality; a group of characteristics that the inner self uses to solve various problems."

"Each of you exists in other realities and other dimensions, and the self that you call yourself is but a small portion of your entire identity."

"Within the self that you know is the prime identity, the whole self. This whole self has lived many lives and adopted many personalities. Personality may be somewhat molded by the circumstances that are created for it by the whole self but the prime identity uses the resulting experience."

"Your prime identity is an energy essence personality which is composed of energy gestalts. As each individual consciousness grows, out of its experience it forms other 'personalities' or fragments of itself. These fragments are entirely independent as to action and decision, while constantly in communication with the whole self of which they are a part. These 'fragments' themselves grow, develop, and may form their own entities or 'personality gestalts.''

"You have constant contact with the other parts of your whole self, but your ego is so focused upon physical reality and survival within it that you do not hear the inner voices. No individuality is ever lost. It is always in existence.'

"There is an inner ego, an inner self which organises 'unconscious' material. As the outer ego manipulates within the physical environment, so the inner ego or self organises and manipulates within inner reality."

"It is this inner self, out of massive knowledge and the unlimited scope of its consciousness, that forms the physical world and provides the stimuli to keep the outer ego at the job of awareness. The inner self organises, initiates, projects and controls the transformation of psychic energy into matter and objects."

"The individual inner self, through constant effort of great intensity, cooperates with other entities like itself to form and maintain the physical reality that you know."

"The inner self has a virtually infinite reservoir from which to draw knowledge and experience. All kinds of choices are available, and the diversity of physical matter is a reflection of this deep source and variety."

"Having determined upon physical reality as a dimension in which it will express itself, the inner self, first of all, takes care to form and maintain the physical basis upon which all else must depend — the properties of the earth that can be called the natural ones."

"It is the daily ego's ignorance and limited focus that makes it view so-called unconscious activity as chaotic. The waking ego dealing with physical reality cannot know all the unconscious material directly. The daily ego is simply not conscious enough to be able to contain the vast knowledge that belongs to the inner conscious self from which it springs.

The outer ego is spoon-fed, being given only those feelings and emotions, only that data, that it can handle. This data is presented in a highly specialized manner, usually in terms of information picked up by the physical senses."

"The inner self is not only conscious, but conscious of itself, both as an individuality and as an individuality that is a part of all other consciousness. It is continually aware of both this apartness and unity-with. The outer ego is not continuously aware of this fact. It frequently forgets its 'whole' nature."

"When it becomes swept up in a strong emotion it

seems to lose itself. When it most vigorously maintains its sense of individuality, it is no longer aware of unity-with. If the ego were aware of the constant barrage of telepathic communications that do impinge upon it, it would have a most difficult time retaining a sense of identity."

"You must learn to listen to the voice of the inner self and work with it. You may also simply ask the inner self to make the answers to problems available on a conscious basis."

Thoughts on Dreams

"Humanity dreams the same dream at once, and you have your mass world. The whole construction is like an educational play in which you are the producers as well as the actors. There is a play within a play within a play. There is no end to the "within" of things. The dreamer dreams, and the dreamer within the dream dreams. But the dreams are not meaningless, and the actions within them are significant. The whole self is the observer and the participator in the roles."

"When you dream of others, they know it. When they dream of you, you know it."

"Throughout the ages, some have recognised the fact that there is self-consciousness and purpose in dream and sleep states, and have maintained, even in waking life, the sense of continuity of the inner self. To such people it is no longer possible to completely identify with the ego consciousness. They are too aware of themselves as more. When such knowledge is gained, the ego can accept it, for it finds to its surprise that is not less conscious, but more, and that its limitations are dissipated."

"A man's thoughts and dreams are more far reaching than he knows. They exist in more dimensions; they affect worlds of which he is unaware. They are as concrete, in effect, as any building. The dream world is constructed within a field that you cannot physically perceive, but it has more continuity than the world you know."

"When you are manipulating within physical reality, you have a fairly simple set of rules to serve you. Within dream reality there is greater freedom. Each dream begins with psychic energy which the individual transforms into a reality which is just as functional and real as physical reality."

"Through our dreams we change physical reality, and our physical daily experience alters our dream experience. There is constant interaction. Our consciousness is simply directed in a different kind of reality when we dream, a reality as vivid as waking life."

"On one level the personality attempts to solve problems through dream construction. Dream action can be turned toward fulfilling constructive expectations, which will effect a change for the better!"

"Dreams can be utilised creatively to improve health,

gain inspiration, restore vitality, solve problems and enrich family relationships. You can have a pleasant and joyful dream that will completely restore your good spirits and vitality."

"In our dream life we also visit other levels of existence, and gain needed skills."

"The ego is not present in dream reality. The waking consciousness is not the ego. The ego is only that portion of waking consciousness that deals with physical manipulation.

Waking consciousness can be taken into the dream state, but the ego cannot, as it would falter and cause failure there. When you take your consciousness into the dream state, you will meet with various conditions, some you can manipulate, some you cannot. Some dream locations will be of your own making, and others will be strange to you because they belong to other dimensions of reality."

"As the personality is changed by any experience, it is changed by dreams. We may forget our dreams, but they are always part of us. The dreams experience is felt directly by the inner self. Dreams have their own actuality, they not only exist independent of the dreamer, but they also have tangible form, though not in the form of matter as you are familiar with it. They are forever contained as electrically coded data within the cells of the physical organism."

"The dream universe possesses concepts which will someday completely transform the physical world, but the denial of such concepts as possibilities delays their emergence."

"There are also shared or mass dreams. In these mankind deals with problems of his political and social structure. In these man dreams individually and collectively of ways in which changeabouts could occur. These dreams actually help bring about the resulting change. The very energy and direction of these dreams will help change the situation. The solutions reached are not always the same as those he accepts in the physical world."

"The energy behind a 'bad dream' is the energy of hidden fears, which could be formed by anyone, since there are fears in anyone. Fear directs your conscious energy into the realm of reality of that fear, and you then must deal at that level. The words 'May peace be with you' will get you through any difficulty in other layers of reality."

Thoughts on Death

"In the dawn of physical existence, men knew that death was merely a change of form."

"What you call death is rather your choice to focus in other dimensions and realities. You do not acquire a 'spirit' at death. You are one, now! You adopt a body as a space traveler wears a space suit, and for much the same reason."

"Your idea of space and time is determined by your neurological structure. The camouflage is so craftily executed and created by the inner self that you must, by necessity, focus your attention on the physical reality which has been created."

"Time as you experience it is an illusion caused by your own physical senses. The apparent boundaries between past, present and future are only illusions caused by the amount of action you can physically perceive, and so it seems to you that one moment exists and is gone forever, and the next moment comes and like the one before also disappears."

"Everything in the universe exists at one time simultaneously. The first words ever spoken still ring through the universe, and in your terms, the last words ever spoken has already been said."

"The past, present and future only appear to those who exist within three-dimensional reality. The past exists as a series of electromagnetic connections held in the physical brain and in the nonphysical mind. These electromagnetic connections can be changed."

"The future consists of a series of electromagnetic connections in the mind and brain also. In other words, the past and present are real to the same extent. You take it for granted that present action can change the future, but present actions can also change the past."

"The past is no more objective or independent from the perceiver than is the present. The electromagnetic connections were largely made by the individual perceiver. The connection can be changed, and such changes are far from uncommon. These changes happen spontaneously on a subconscious basis."

"The past is seldom what you remember it to be, for you have already rearranged it from the instant of any given event. The past is being constantly re-created by each individual as attitudes and associations change.

This is an actual recreation, not a symbolic one. The child is indeed still within the man, but he is not the child that 'was', for even the child within the man constantly changes."

"Every action changes every other action. Therefore, every action in your present affects actions you call past. It is possible to react in the past to an event that has not occurred, and to be influenced by your own future."

"It is also possible for an individual to react in the past to an event in the future, which in your terms, may never occur."

"Because past, present and future exist simultaneously, there is no reason why you cannot react to an event whether or not it happens to fall within the small field of reality in which you usually observe and participate."

"On a subconscious level, you react to many events

that have not yet occurred as far as your ego's awareness is concerned. Such reactions are carefully screened out and not admitted to consciousness. The ego finds such instances distracting and annoying, and when forced to admit their validity, will resort to the most far fetched rationalizations to explain them."

"No event is predestined. Any given event can be changed not only before and during but after its occurrence. The individual is hardly at the mercy of past events, for he changes them constantly. He is hardly at the mercy of future events, for he changes these not only before but after their happening. An individuals future actions are not dependent upon a concrete finished past, for such a past never existed."

"The past is as real as the future, no more or less. There is a part of you that is not locked within physical reality, and that part of you knows that there is only an Eternal Now. The part of you that knows is the whole self, your inner and outer ego (all that you are)."

Thoughts on God

"If you prefer, you can call the supreme psychic gestalt God, but you should not attempt to objectify him. What you call God is the sum of all consciousness, and yet the whole is more than the sum of its parts."

"(It) is not one individual, but an energy gestalt. (It) is a psychic pyramid of interrelated, ever expanding consciousness that creates simultaneous and instantaneously, universes and individuals that are given duration, psychic comprehension, intelligence and eternal validity. Its energy is so unbelievable that is does indeed from all universes; and because its energy is within and behind all universes, fields and systems, it is indeed aware of each sparrow that falls, for it is each sparrow that falls."

"Dimly remembered through what you would call history, there was a state of agony in which the powers of creativity and existence were known, but the ways to produce them were not known. All That Is existed in a state of being, but without the means to find expression for its being.

All That Is had to learn this lesson, and could not be taught. From this agony, creativity was originally drawn, and its reflection is still seen. All That Is retains the memory of that state, and it serves as a constant impetus toward renewed creativity. Desire, wish and expectation, therefore, rule all actions and are the basis for all realities. Within the dreams of All That Is, potential beings had consciousness before any beginning as you know it."

"All That Is saw an infinity of probable, conscious individuals. These probable individual selves found themselves alive within a God's dream and they clamoured to be released into actuality. All That Is yearned to release them and sought within itself for the means to do so.

Finally, with love and longing it let go of that portion of itself, and they were free. The psychic energy exploded in a flash of creation."

"All That Is loves all that it has created down to the least, for It realises the dearness and uniqueness of each consciousness which has been wrest from such a state of agony. It is triumphant and joyful at each development taken by each consciousness, and it revels and takes joy in the slightest creative act of each of its issues."

"All individuals remember their source, and now dream of All That Is as It once dreamed of them. And they yearn toward that immense source... and yearn to give it actuality through their own creations."

"The connections between you and All That Is can never be severed, and its awareness is so delicate and focused that its attention is indeed directed with a prime creator's love to each consciousness."

"All That Is knows no other. It does not know whether or not other psychic gestalts like itself may exist. It is constantly searching."

"There are answers to some questions that I cannot give you about the origin of All That Is, for they are not known anywhere in the system in which we have our existence."

"All portions of All That Is are constantly changing. All

that is constantly seeking to know itself, for seeking itself is a creative activity and the core of all action."

"You, as a consciousness, seek to know yourself and become aware of yourself as a distinct individual portion of All That Is. You automatically draw on the overall energy of All That Is, since your existence is dependent upon it. The portion of All That Is that is aware of itself as you, that is focused within your existence, can be called upon for help when necessary. This portion of All That Is looks out for your interests and may be called upon in a personal manner. A psychic gestalt may seem impersonal to you, but its energy forms your person."

■

9

The Art of Living Foundation and Courses for Good Living

The Art of Living Foundation is a non-profit, volunteer based organisation founded by Sri Sri Ravi Shankar. A non-denominational, educational and humanitarian non-profit organisation, The Art of Living Foundation mission statement is to uplift society by strengthening the individual through programmes that create a sense of belonging, restore human values, develop life to its full potential, and encourage people from all backgrounds, religions, and cultural traditions to come together in celebration and service.

According to the Foundation, it has programmes in more than 140 countries around the world, and offers several courses to bring individuals knowledge and techniques to unlock their deepest potential and bring fullness to life.

159

Sri Sri Ravi Shankar and his Philosophy for Good Life

Sri Sri Ravi Shankar is a spiritual and humanitarian leader. He was born on May 13, 1956 in Tamil Nadu, India. He is often referred to by the double-honorific "Sri Sri", Guruji or Gurudev. He is the founder of the International Art of Living Foundation which aims to relieve stress at an individual level, and to relieve disease and violence at a societal level. Sri Sri is also a driving force behind the charitable organisation, International Association for Human Values, which conducts the "5H" programme.

According to Art of Living Foundation, even though the world is a mixture of happiness and sorrow, it shouldn't deter any one from seeking enjoyment in whatever one does. Sri Sri Ravi Shankar elucidates, "It is written in the Upanishads, the *Atman*, *soul*, is *Satchidanandamaya* (complete bliss). Spirituality is not boring. It is the *Rasa* (flavour) of life."

This blissful state can only be attained when one follows the religion of humanity, *Manav Dharma*, by spreading love in each human soul. Sri Sri Ravi Shankar has even unfolded the path to this state, simply follow it: "How far to Heaven? Just open your eyes and look. You are in Heaven."

Philosophy and Activities

Sri Sri emphasises breath as the link between body and mind and therefore a tool to relax the mind. He also emphasises service to others, besides meditating. According to him, science and spirituality are linked and consistent. His stated vision is to create a world which is free of stress and violence through acquisition of wisdom, and his programmes aim to offer practical tools to accomplish wisdom. In his view, "Truth is spherical rather than linear; so it has to be contradictory." "Anything that is spherical is always contradictory," says Sri Sri.

Sudarshan Kriya

Sudarshan Kriya is the core component of the Art of Living courses. Persons enrolling for the courses are required to sign non-disclosure agreements, so that specifics of the Sudarshan Kriya technique are not made public.

Sudarshan Kriya is said to infuse the body with energy and harmonise the natural rhythms of the body, mind, and emotions. There have been several independent studies published on the effects of the technique.

Sudarshan Kriya is a unique rhythmical breathing process that is said to have been revealed to Sri Sri Ravi Shankar during a spell of silent meditation that he had gone into for 10 days in 1982. The theory is that the kriya allows a healthy and pleasant mind to produce  chemical messengers, which travel from the nervous system to the immune system, resulting in the overall betterment of both body and mind.

Process

This kriya, as done at the Art of Living workshops, involves regulating one's breath to the sounds of So-hum ('So' for inhale and 'hum' for exhale) coming from the tape recorder in Sri Sri Ravi Shankar's voice. The entire kriya involves multiple rounds with each round having long, medium and short inhalation and exhalations with varying rhythms and intensities.

Sri Sri Ravi Shankar has described the working of the Sudarshan Kriya thus:

- "There is a rhythm in nature. Seasons come and go. In your own body also, there is a rhythm. Life has a particular rhythm. Similarly, your breath also goes in a pattern. Your emotions move in a particular rhythm, as well as your thoughts. All these rhythms arise from your being, which has its own rhythm.

- "In Sudarshan Kriya, we get into the rhythm of our being and see how our being is permeating our emotions, our thoughts, our breath and our bodies. Soon, every cell of our body becomes alive and releases all the toxins and negative emotions it has stored from times past. Once again, we are able to smile from our hearts."

Sudarshan Kriya is accompanied by certain other breathing techniques like Ujjayi Pranayama and the

Bhastrika Pranayama, which proponents claim help in quelling the turmoil of the mind. According to Sri Sri Ravi Shankar, through this kriya the mind experiences deep rest. He states that the process also involves the infusion of a maximum amount of oxygen to the cells, which helps in the release of neuropeptides that regularise Abnormal Brain Wave patterns in patients suffering from neural disorders.

Enlightenment for Good Living

Enlightenment is the very core of our being; going into the core of our self and living our life from there. We all came into this world gifted with innocence, but gradually, as we became more intelligent, we lost our innocence. We were born with silence, and as we grew up, we lost the silence and were filled with words. We lived in our hearts, and as time passed, we moved into our heads. Now the reversal of this journey is enlightenment. It is the journey from head back to the heart, from words, back to silence; getting back to our innocence in spite of our intelligence. Although very simple, this is a great achievement. Knowledge should lead you to that beautiful point of "I don't know."

The purpose of knowledge is ignorance. The completion of knowledge will lead you to amazement and wonder. It makes you aware of this existence. Mysteries are to be lived, not understood. One can live life so fully in its completeness, in its totality. Enlightenment is that state of being so mature and unshakable by any circumstance. Come what may, nothing can rob the smile from your heart. Not identifying with limited boundaries and feeling "all that exists in this universe belongs to me," this is enlightenment. Enlightenment is that state of being so mature and unshakable by any circumstance. Come what may, nothing can rob the smile from your heart.

Unenlightenment is easy to define. It is limiting yourself by saying, "I belong to this particular place," or "I am from that culture." It's like children saying, "My dad is better than your dad," or "My toy is better than your toy." I think most people around the world are stuck in that mental age group. Just the toys have changed. Adults say, "My country is better than your country." A Christian will say, "The Bible is truth," and a Hindu will say, "The Vedas are truth. They are very ancient." Muslims will say, "The Koran is the last word of God." We attribute glory to something just because we are from that culture, not for what it is. If one could take credit for all that exists throughout the ages and feel as though "it belongs to me," then that is maturity. "This is my wealth because I belong to the Divine."

The Divine, according to time and space, gave different knowledge in different places. One becomes the knower of the whole universe and sees that, "all the beautiful flowers are all from my garden." The whole evolution of man is from being somebody to being nobody, and from being nobody to being everybody. Have you observed that young children have that sense of belonging, that oneness, that innocence? As we grew up we lost that innocence and became more cunning. The innocence of an ignorant man has no value, and the cunningness of an intelligent man also has no value. Enlightenment is a rare combination of innocence and intelligence, with words to express and, at the same time, being very silent. In that state, the mind is fully in the present moment. Whatever is necessary is revealed to you in such a natural and spontaneous way. You just sit and the song flows through you.

Dealing with Fear

One definite thing in life is that everyone is going to die. No one can escape this reality. The only difference is that some people may die a little sooner and some a little later. The doctor dies as well as the patient. The king dies as well as the servant. This is a place where everyone dies.

No one knows how or when they are going to die. If you look at the situation in third world countries, people live in extremely unstable conditions. They are never sure how close death is. There may be a flood or famine or even an epidemic. Monsoons may destroy their homes and the entire family can be uprooted. But still, these people are able to smile and enjoy the life that they have. The quality of our life is very important. The intensity with which we live from moment to moment is essential. Sickness has nothing to do with death. It is the fear associated with having a disease that disturbs and weakens one's whole system. A clear mind free of fear can have a healing effect on the body. So, how do we get over this fear?

First, there is an observation: Observe the fear. When

fear comes, what happens? A sensation arises in the chest region of the body. Observe this sensation and go deep into it. You see, every emotion in the mind creates a corresponding sensation in the body. When you observe sensations, emotions are transformed as sensations in the body and then they disappear. The sensations are released and the mind becomes clear.

If this is too difficult and is not possible to do without some help, then secondly, you can have a sense of belonging. You belong to God, to the universe, or to some power. God is taking care of me, my master is taking care of me, the Divine is taking care of me. This sense of belonging is an easier and simpler way to deal with fear.

If this sense of belonging is not possible, then see the impermanence of life. Everything is changing around you. You cannot hold on to anything. Things come and things go. Emotions change, behaviors change, everything changes. The world is changing all around you. See the impermanence in everything. You will gain strength from this understanding and the fear will also disappear.

Fear is clinging to something, holding on and not letting go. But there is nothing you can hold onto in this life. One day you have to bid goodbye to everything, absolutely everything, including your very own body. This awareness brings an enormous strength from within.

Just as the root cause of fear can be eliminated through understanding and observation, health can be regained by attending to the source of the mind, pure consciousness. Pure consciousness is pure love, and love is the highest healer on the planet. You can say it is your natural self. Love is not an emotion. It is your very existence. It is what you are made up of. To know this, you must be free of fear and anxiety.

The Sanskrit word for health (*swasta*), actually means "stabilised in one's Self." Health means being centred. When the mind is free of fear, free of guilt, free of anger, and more centred, then it can heal the system of any ailment. There is a huge power in consciousness. When you are truly centred, nothing can disturb you. If you throw a small stone in a pond of water, there will be great turbulence, whereas a lake needs a bigger stone to create turbulence. However, nothing can disturb the ocean. Mountains can fall in the ocean, but the ocean remains as it is.

The Art of Good Living: Vipassana Meditation

Everyone seeks peace and harmony, because this is what we lack in our lives. From time to time we all experience agitation, irritation, disharmony. And when we suffer from these miseries, we don't keep them to ourselves; we often distribute them to others as well. Unhappiness permeates the atmosphere around someone who is miserable, and those who come in contact with such a person also become affected. Certainly this is not a skilful way to live.

We ought to live at peace with ourselves, and at peace with others. After all, human beings are social beings, having to live in society and deal with each other. But how are we to live peacefully? How are we to remain harmonious within, and maintain peace and harmony around us, so that others can also live peacefully and harmoniously?

In order to be relieved of our misery, we have to know the basic reason for it, the cause of the suffering. If we investigate the problem, it becomes clear that whenever we start generating any negativity or impurity in the mind, we are bound to become unhappy. A negativity in the mind, a mental defilement or impurity, cannot coexist with peace and harmony.

How do we start generating negativity? Again, by investigation, it becomes clear. We become unhappy when we find someone behaving in a way that we don't like, or when we find something happening which we don't like. Unwanted things happen and we create tension within. Wanted things do not happen, some obstacle comes in the way, and again we create tension within; we start tying knots within. And throughout life, unwanted things keep on happening, wanted things may or may not happen, and this process of reaction, of tying knots makes the entire mental and physical structure so tense, so full of negativity, that life becomes miserable.

Now, one way to solve this problem is to arrange that nothing unwanted happens in life, that everything keeps on happening exactly as we desire. Either we must develop the power, or somebody else who will come to our aid must have the power, to see that unwanted things do not happen and that everything we want happens. But this is impossible. There is no one in the world whose desires are always fulfilled, in whose life everything happens according to his or her wishes, without anything unwanted happening. Things constantly occur that are contrary to our desires and wishes. So the question arises: how can we stop reacting blindly when confronted with things that we don't like? How can we stop creating tension and remain peaceful and harmonious?

In India, as well as in other countries, wise saintly persons of the past studied this problem—the problem of human suffering—and found a solution: if something unwanted happens and you start to react by generating anger, fear or any negativity, then, as soon as possible, you should divert your attention to something else. For example, get up, take a glass of water, start drinking— your anger won't multiply; on the other hand, it'll begin to subside. Or start counting: one, two, three, four. Or start repeating a word, or a phrase, or some mantra, perhaps the name of a god or saintly person towards whom you have devotion; the mind is diverted, and to some extent you'll be free of the negativity, free of the anger.

This solution was helpful; it worked. It still works. Responding like this, the mind feels free from agitation. However, the solution works only at the conscious level. In fact, by diverting the attention you push the negativity deep into the unconscious, and there you continue to generate and multiply the same defilement. On the surface there is a layer of peace and harmony, but in the depths of the mind there is a sleeping volcano of suppressed negativity which sooner or later may erupt in a violent explosion.

Other explorers of inner truth went still further in their search and, by experiencing the reality of mind and matter within themselves, recognised that diverting the attention is only running away from the problem. Escape is no solution; you have to face the problem. Whenever negativity arises in the mind, just observe it, face it. As soon as you start to observe a mental impurity, it begins to lose its strength and slowly withers away.

A good solution; it avoids both extremes—suppression and expression. Burying the negativity in the unconscious will not eradicate it, and allowing it to manifest as unwholesome physical or vocal actions will only create more problems. But if you just observe, then the defilement passes away and you are free of it.

This sounds wonderful, but is it really practical? It's not easy to face one's own impurities. When anger arises, it so quickly overwhelms us that we don't even notice. Then, overpowered by anger, we perform physical or vocal actions which harm ourselves and others. Later, when the anger has passed, we start crying and repenting, begging pardon from this or that person or from God: "Oh, I made a mistake, please excuse me!" But the next time we are in a similar situation, we again react in the same way. This continual repenting doesn't help at all.

The difficulty is that we are not aware when negativity starts. It begins deep in the unconscious mind, and by the time it reaches the conscious level it has gained so much strength that it overwhelms us, and we cannot observe it.

However, someone who reached the ultimate truth

found a real solution. He discovered that whenever any impurity arises in the mind, physically two things start happening simultaneously. One is that the breath loses its normal rhythm. We start breathing harder whenever negativity comes into the mind. This is easy to observe. At a subtler level, a biochemical reaction starts in the body, resulting in some sensation. Every impurity will generate some sensation or the other within the body.

This presents a practical solution. An ordinary person cannot observe abstract defilements of the mind—abstract fear, anger or passion. But with proper training and practice it is very easy to observe respiration and body sensations, both of which are directly related to mental defilements.

Respiration and sensations will help in two ways. First, they will be like private secretaries. As soon as a negativity arises in the mind, the breath will lose its normality; it will start shouting, "Look, something has gone wrong!" And we cannot scold the breath; we have to accept the warning. Similarly, the sensations will tell us that something has gone wrong. Then, having been warned, we can start observing the respiration, start observing the sensations, and very quickly we find that the negativity passes away.

This mental-physical phenomenon is like a coin with two sides. On one side are the thoughts and emotions arising in the mind, on the other side are the respiration and sensations in the body. Any thoughts or emotions, any mental impurities that arise manifest themselves in the breath and the sensations of that moment. Thus, by observing the respiration or the sensations, we are in fact observing mental impurities. Instead of running away from the problem, we are facing reality as it is. As a result, we discover that these impurities lose their strength; they no longer overpower us as they did in the past. If we persist, they eventually disappear altogether and we begin to live a peaceful and happy life, a life increasingly free of negativities.

In this way the technique of self-observation shows us reality in its two aspects, inner and outer. Previously we only looked outward, missing the inner truth. We always looked outside for the cause of our unhappiness; we always blamed and tried to change the reality outside. Being ignorant of the inner reality, we never understood that the cause of suffering lies within, in our own blind reactions toward pleasant and unpleasant sensations.

Now, with training, we can see the other side of the coin. We can be aware of our breathing and also of what is happening inside. Whatever it is, breath or sensation, we learn just to observe it without losing our mental balance. We stop reacting and multiplying our misery. Instead, we allow the defilements to manifest and pass away.

The more one practices this technique, the more quickly negativities will dissolve. Gradually the mind becomes free of defilements, becomes pure. A pure mind is always full of love—selfless love for all others, full of compassion for the failings and sufferings of others, full of joy at their success and happiness, full of equanimity in the face of any situation.

When one reaches this stage, the entire pattern of one's life changes. It is no longer possible to do anything vocally or physically which will disturb the peace and happiness of others. Instead, a balanced mind not only becomes peaceful, but the surrounding atmosphere also becomes permeated with peace and harmony, and this will start affecting others, helping others too.

By learning to remain balanced in the face of everything experienced inside, one develops detachment towards all that one encounters in external situations as well. However, this detachment is not escapism or indifference to the problems of the world. Those who regularly practice Vipassana become more sensitive to the sufferings of others, and do their utmost to relieve suffering in whatever way they can—not with any agitation, but with a mind full of love, compassion and equanimity. They learn holy indifference—how to be fully committed, fully involved in helping others, while at the same time maintaining balance of mind. In this way they remain peaceful and happy, while working for the peace and happiness of others.

This is what the Buddha taught: an art of living. He never established or taught any religion, any "ism". He never instructed those who came to him to practice any rites or rituals, any empty formalities. Instead, he taught them just to observe nature as it is, by observing the reality inside. Out of ignorance we keep reacting in ways which harm ourselves and others. But when wisdom arises—the wisdom of observing reality as it is—this habit of reacting falls away. When we cease to react blindly, then we are capable of real action—action proceeding from a balanced mind, a mind which sees and understands the truth. Such action can only be positive, creative, helpful to ourselves and to others.

What is necessary, then, is to "know thyself"—advice which every wise person has given. We must know ourselves, not just intellectually in the realm of ideas and theories, and not just emotionally or devotionally, simply accepting blindly what we have heard or read. Such knowledge is not enough. Rather, we must know reality experientially. We must experience directly the reality of this mental-physical phenomenon. This alone is what will help us be free of our suffering.

This direct experience of our own inner reality, this technique of self-observation, is what is called Vipassana meditation. In the language of India in the time of the Buddha, *passana* meant seeing in the ordinary way, with one's eyes open; but *vipassana* is observing things as they actually are, not just as they appear to be. Apparent truth has to be penetrated, until we reach the ultimate truth of the entire psycho-physical structure. When we experience this truth, then we learn to stop reacting blindly, to stop creating negativities—and naturally the old ones are gradually eradicated. We become liberated from misery and experience true happiness.

There are three steps to the training given in a meditation course. First, one must abstain from any action, physical or vocal, which disturbs the peace and harmony of others. One cannot work to liberate oneself from impurities of the mind while at the same time continuing to perform deeds of body and speech which only multiply them. Therefore, a code of morality is the essential first step of the practice. One undertakes not to kill, not to steal, not to commit sexual misconduct, not to tell lies, and not to use intoxicants. By abstaining from such actions, one allows the mind to quiet down sufficiently in order to proceed further.

The next step is to develop some mastery over this wild mind by training it to remain fixed on a single object, the breath. One tries to keep one's attention on the respiration for as long as possible. This is not a breathing exercise; one does not regulate the breath. Instead, one observes natural respiration as it is, as it comes in, as it goes out. In this way one further calms the mind so that it is no longer overpowered by intense negativities. At the same time, one is concentrating the mind, making it sharp and penetrating, capable of the work of insight.

These first two steps, living a moral life, and controlling the mind, are very necessary and beneficial in themselves, but they will lead to suppression of negativities unless one takes the third step: purifying the mind of defilements by developing insight into one's own nature. This is Vipassana: experiencing one's own reality by the systematic and dispassionate observation within oneself of the ever-changing mind-matter phenomenon manifesting itself as sensations. This is the culmination of the teaching of the Buddha: self-purification by self-observation.

It can be practiced by one and all. Everyone faces the

problem of suffering. It is a universal malady which requires a universal remedy, not a sectarian one. When one suffers from anger, it's not Buddhist anger, Hindu anger, or Christian anger. Anger is anger. When one becomes agitated as a result of this anger, this agitation is not Christian, or Jewish, or Muslim. The malady is universal. The remedy must also be universal.

Vipassana is such a remedy. No one will object to a code of living which respects the peace and harmony of others. No one will object to developing control over the mind. No one will object to developing insight into one's own nature, by which it is possible to free the mind of negativities. Vipassana is a universal path.

Observing reality as it is by observing the truth inside— this is knowing oneself directly and experientially. As one practices, one keeps freeing oneself from the misery of mental impurities. From the gross, external, apparent truth, one penetrates to the ultimate truth of mind and matter. Then one transcends that, and experiences a truth which is beyond mind and matter, beyond time and space, beyond the conditioned field of relativity: the truth of total liberation from all defilements, all impurities, all suffering. Whatever name one gives this ultimate truth is irrelevant; it is the final goal of everyone.

■